The Warden's Son
Growing up at the Idaho State Penitentiary

By Jerry Clapp

Hidden Shelf Publishing House
P.O. Box 4168, McCall, ID 83638
www.hiddenshelfpublishinghouse.com

Editors: Rachel Wickstrom, Megan Whitfield

Research: Anthony Parry

Graphic design: Kristen Carrico (front cover), Allison Kaukola (back cover)

Interior layout: Kerstin Stokes

ISBN: 978-1-7354145-2-2

Publisher's Cataloging-in-Publication data

Names: Clapp, Jerry, author.
Title: The warden's son : growing up at the Idaho State Penitentiary
Penitentiary / by Jerry Clapp.
Description: Includes bibliographical references and index. | McCall, ID:
Hidden Shelf Publishing House, 2020.
Identifiers: LCCN: 2020919958 | ISBN: 978-1-7354145-2-2
Subjects: LCSH Clapp, Jerry. | Idaho State Penitentiary--History.
| Corrections--Idaho--History. | Correctional institutions--Idaho-
-History. | Prisoners--Idaho--Biography. | BISAC BIOGRAPHY &
AUTOBIOGRAPHY / Personal Memoirs | TRUE CRIME / Historical
Classification: LCC HV9475.I252 .C53 2020 | DDC 365.6/097/092--dc23

Printed in the United States of America

Table of Contents

For many years, Jerry Clapp told his children and grand-children the stories of growing up at the Idaho State Penitentiary. Late in life, he was encouraged by his family to write down his remembrances . . .

Foreward

The Idaho Territorial Penitentiary in Boise opened its doors in the spring of 1872. In the beginning, the penitentiary consisted of a single three-tiered cell house that could hold forty men for the entire territory of Idaho. A United States marshal, appointed by the president, fulfilled the position of warden until Idaho entered the Union in 1890. After that, the position was appointed by the governor. Wardens included politicians, policemen, lawyers, soldiers, and even a chaplain until the site was officially closed in 1973. The most notable of these wardens in the prison's history was Louis E. Clapp, who served from 1945-1966.

As an interpretive specialist at the Old Idaho State Penitentiary, I've dedicated my time to researching the history of the site, the lives of more than 13,000 men and women who resided here, and the prison administrators and guards who kept watch over Idaho's most dangerous criminals.

I first encountered Jerry Clapp—Louis Clapp's only son—while digitizing oral histories in 2014. Jerry had sat down with site historians in 1982 and again in 1987 to recount his life growing up on prison grounds as the son of a prison warden. I never had the pleasure of meeting him before his death in 2015, but I became captivated by his stories.

I was thrilled when Hidden Shelf Publishing House contacted me with questions regarding this posthumous memoir. The questions began simply enough by asking about proper spellings of the names of guards and inmates, as Jerry was not known for his handwriting. After a few spellings were cleared up, I received more inquiries about certain inmates and guards that Jerry references in his writings. This unveiled a trove of stories that had previously been lost to time, not recorded in newspapers or official records.

Jerry effectively chronicles the life of the warden's family living on the grounds of the penitentiary by witnessing escapes, executions, trials, and even developing close bonds with notorious criminals. He interacted daily with men serving long sentences who prepared his meals, trimmed his hair, and taught him life lessons in their own unique ways. Jerry's stories display humanity in a place known for punishment and brutality.

Jerry's father began his career in Idaho law enforcement. Lou Clapp served as a Wallace city patrolman, the chief deputy sheriff in Shoshone County, and an officer with the Idaho state police. In late 1944, he was the youngest man ever to be appointed warden of the state penitentiary and he would hold the position longer than any other warden in the prison's history.

Warden was a political position appointed by the prison board, which consisted of the governor, secretary of state, and the attorney general of Idaho. Louis Clapp, a Democrat, served under five governors (two Democrats and three Republicans). During each election season, the Clapp family braced for the possibility that Lou would be ousted for a new head of the prison, but because of his record and character, the prison board retained him in the post. He only resigned to continue his public service as Idaho's Secretary of State in 1966. By all accounts, both as a father and a prison warden, Louis was beloved for his dedication to his position and his steadfast honesty. He was a straight shooter and a man of his word. During the nearly 22-year period that Warden Clapp held office, the prison saw vast improvements in the facility and quality of life for inmates. These included an expansion in rehabilitative programs, the development of the Idaho State Board of Corrections, the development of several inmate led clubs, and improvements in prison farm crop yields. At the end of World War II, Clapp spearheaded the construction of two new cell houses, avoiding problems in the late 1950s when the population of the site peaked at more than 500 convicts.

Warden Clapp further enhanced trusty programs that enabled

model inmates to be trusted with special tasks and given more freedoms than other inmates. He wasn't focused on keeping men locked in cells, but on rehabilitation and providing them with vocational training for their inevitable release back into society.

Clapp was essential in finding the site of the current correctional institution, working with prison administrators in the construction of a modern facility.

Jerry Clapp followed in his father's footsteps and dedicated his life to Idaho law and public service. He became the clerk of the U.S. Courts in the District of Idaho, a position he held until his retirement.

This memoir explores the lives of an entire family living on the edge of potential danger. It provides insight into the inner workings of the prison. It exemplifies the strength required to lead a prison and make a true impact to many lives.

> – Anthony Parry, Interpretive Specialist, Idaho
> State Historical Society

Map of Idaho State Penitentiary (1958)

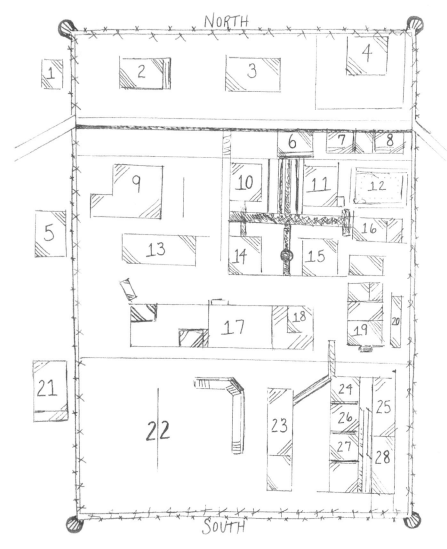

1- Warden's Residence
2- Guards' Dorm
3- Guards' Dorm
4- Women's Ward
5- Administration Building
6- Entrance Building
7- Commissary
8- Trusties' Dorm
9- Detention Cell House #5
10- Cell House #2
11- Cell House #1
12- Rose garden
13- Cell House #4
14- Cell House #3
15- Chapel
16- Dining Hall
17- Loafing Area
18- Bakery
19- Hospital
20- Solitary Cell House
21- Heating Plant
22- Recreation Field
23- License Plate Factory
24- Print Shop
25- Auditorium
26- Auto & Sheet Metal Shop
27- Machine & Welding Shop
28- School

Entrance to the Idaho State Penitentiary. (Idaho State Archives)

Chapter 1

Welcome to the Penitentiary

The huge house was quiet and cold, a light snow falling outside. It was January 9, 1945, my first night in this unfamiliar place. I rolled over from a deep sleep, curling up against the chill that pervaded the air in the bedroom, a draft from the door purposely left ajar. I tried to pull the blankets up to my face, but was met with resistance, a weight holding them down. Pal, our border collie, was asleep at my feet, unmoved by my adjustments. I was 10 years old, so I welcomed the security of his presence. His body warmth was comforting in the drafty old house my family would now call home. I hunkered down into the blankets rather than trying to pull them up.

Suddenly, a sound unlike anything I had ever heard jerked me awake. My eyes flew open as a loud siren screamed just outside my window. Huge bright lights shone directly into the room, casting terrifying shadows on the walls. The tree outside my window had no leaves, just sharp, angry looking branches that appeared to be reaching in to grab me from my bed. Without a curtain covering the window, the shadows splashed across the wall, making the darkest corners a pitch black. The light between the stark cage-like shadows was bright and unforgiving against the mostly empty room. I was terrified.

The bare walls echoed the sound of the siren. It was deafening. I could hear men shouting and running on the snow-covered road outside the house. I realized that the siren was an emergency signal; one or more prisoners had probably escaped. Pal, my great protector, was cowering on the bed, quietly whimpering with his ears perked up and eyes nervously looking around the room. I was stiff as a board, horrible scenarios dashing through my head.

With the siren still screaming, men's voices seemed to be growing louder. *What do I do?* I thought to myself while I searched for the safest looking place in the room. *Do I hide?* These thoughts rapidly circled in my brain. However, I suddenly felt conflicted. I was scared, but also curious. *Maybe I should get up and peek through the window.* Frozen in my bed, I heard a creaking floorboard outside of my room. The light from the hallway—which I purposely left on all night—now cast a looming shadow that seemed to creep across the bedroom floor.

It was too late to hide; the escaped prisoner was outside my room, coming to get me. The sliver of light from the hallway was no longer visible as the figure moved closer to my door. I jumped, yanking the covers over my head. I was curled into a ball as close to Pal as I could be. I hardly dared to breathe, my racing heart feeling as if it was about to burst. Pal didn't make a sound either.

"Come on, Jerry," my dad commanded. "Put your shoes on. We have to go. It's best we leave Pal here."

The panic ebbed away as I climbed out of the bed.

"No time for boots," Dad said. "Put on your slippers and coat. You'll be indoors in a moment."

We left the house through the front door, locking the dog behind us. I could finally see the scene; guards running back and forth, some of them armed. I could hear shouts from all over the grounds and from as far away as the foothills. There was an escaped convict.

Dad hurried me toward his office in the administration building. "You'll be safe here," he said. "The door will be locked and I'll have men stationed outside the door. I'll be back."

My dad, the newly appointed warden of the Idaho State Penitentiary, stormed out of the building to lead a chase into the darkness. This was his responsibility now. I sat there alone, trembling in silence with the snow melting from my slippers. I was thankful my mother and younger sister were not yet here. If they only knew what was happening, they just might want to stay up north. I knew my life would be turned upside down when we moved to this new job, in this new place, surrounded by a lot of dangerous criminals. I just didn't expect all hell would break loose on our first night. Perhaps it was the change in leadership that prompted the escape. Maybe the inmates thought that because dad was the youngest warden the prison had ever seen, they could capitalize on the opportunity.

I thought about Pal, probably hiding under my bed, still frightened. And then I worried about Dad. *I'm safe, but who is protecting him?*

Eventually, the siren stopped. Dad and a group of guards, walked past the office door with an inmate, handcuffed and looking disgruntled. My dad was speaking sternly to him. I couldn't hear his words, but the look on his face and the tone sounded familiar enough for me to know Dad was displeased with the situation. A short time later, Dad unlocked his office and I jumped up from the chair.

"Let's get you back to the house," Dad said in a tired voice.

He explained that a guard would walk me home and wait in the house. Dad had to stay in his office for a while, finishing some business involving the attempted escape. I nodded, ready to be back in my bed with Pal at my side.

The guard assigned to escort me home walked with me through the snow. When we opened the front door, Pal was waiting patiently for me to return. The guard stayed downstairs by the door while I went up to my room, Pal leading the way. I took off my wool coat and snow-soaked slippers. My pajamas felt cold against the sheets as I clambered back into bed. It was dark again, very dark. As Pal made himself comfortable in his usual spot, I felt restless, the depths of my imagination pounding at my brain. *What if more than one man escaped and they only caught one?* I attempted to shake the scary thoughts from my mind, trying not to think of what or who might be hiding in the gloomiest corners of my room. Suddenly, I heard a gentle knock on my door.

"Jerry, will you be able to go back to sleep, son?"

Warden's Residence. (Photo: Idaho State Archives)

Warden Lou Clapp. (Photo: Courtesy of the Clapp Family)

Chapter 2

The Road to Warden

Louis Egmer Clapp was born on May 26, 1909 in Mountain Home, Idaho. He was raised on a farm in Grand View, along the Snake River in the High Desert of southern Idaho. Not unlike myself, Dad was a big, strong, and tall kid. He was also tough.

After the eighth grade, he left home and headed north to Stibnite, a booming Idaho mining district in the mountains of the Payette National Forest. Earning a good income through manual labor in the mines, he sent his paychecks back home to help his family with the farm.

While working in Stibnite, my dad happened to meet my mother, Margaret "Robb" Robbins. They began a traditional romance for the time, got married, and had me, Gerold Louis Clapp ("Jerry") on April 6, 1934. I was born in Boise, even though I prefer to think of myself as a Stibnite local. Dad continued working in the mines for a few more years, until his professional interests took a more authoritative turn. Contacting Fred Taylor, the prosecuting attorney of Valley County, Dad sought counsel on becoming a policeman. At that time, the State Police were governed by the political party in power. Judge Taylor didn't think my dad's prospects were too good, simply because the governor, Barzilla Clark, was a Democrat and Taylor a Republican. Fortunately, Dad's Democratic leanings must have been made clear.

In 1937, Louis E. Clapp became a state trooper and was transferred to northern Idaho where they were having serious mine disputes. Because of his tall stature and commanding demeanor, they believed he could help calm the violent altercations.

At first, we lived in a port of entry station between Mullen and the Idaho-Montana border, along what is now Highway 10. His first assignment in law enforcement was to check trucks coming and going from the port of entry, reviewing licenses, and permits. Now and then, he was called to assist closer to the mines and help keep the rabble-rousing to a minimum.

In those years, the state police were at the mercy of the political structure. Whenever the governor changed, so did the state troopers. When the Republicans regained power in the state, Dad was out of work. Using his connections with other local law officers, he became a policeman in the northern Idaho city of Wallace. When an opportunity came along to be the deputy sheriff in Shoshone County, he immediately got the position. Enjoying that career and making a good name for himself in the area, Dad finally moved up to chief deputy sheriff. He also bought a home in Silverton, Idaho. Even though I was very young, I remember moving into the only home we ever owned.

My father was a political man. He liked to help Democrats campaign and did whatever else he could to support his political party. Leading up to the Idaho election of 1944, my dad assisted in the Gubernatorial campaign for Charlie Gossett. As was customary during the elections, Gossett promised Shoshone County Sheriff Archie McPhale a position with the state government if he could carry the northern part of the state for him. On a campaign trip to Shoshone County, McPhale and my dad arranged for Gossett to meet all the miners leaving work after a long hard day below ground. Greatly respecting the sheriff and deputy sheriff, the miners each took their turn to shake hands with Gossett despite their exhaustion. Gossett would win the north and the state. Shortly after the inauguration, the new governor contacted McPhale to join him in Boise for a state position.

"No disrespect, Governor," McPhale remembered saying. "I don't want to come to Boise. Why don't you give the commitment to my chief deputy, Lou Clapp?"

Governor Gossett invited my father for a meeting at the State Capitol in Boise. Dad was hoping for an appointment as liquor commissioner or head of the state police. However, impressed with my dad's stature and authoritative methods as a deputy sheriff, Gossett immediately offered him the job as warden of the Idaho State Penitentiary.

Although he was not especially thrilled with his new appointment and the stress it no doubt carried, Dad came home to Silverton and told us the news. We figured he would be there for two years, maybe four. Wardens at the Idaho State Penitentiary had been coming and going in a rather rapid fashion. Most wardens were removed because of politics—a new governor meant a new warden. Some had been fired because of corruption; there was a strong temptation to steal from the commissary and take prison property. One former warden mentioned being exhausted by the responsibility of the job.

At the time of his acceptance, little did any of us know that Dad would be warden for more than 21 years. I firmly believe he maintained his wardenship for such a long period of time because of his constant interaction with important politicians and the credibility he built and maintained; not only with politicians, but with inmates and staff at the penitentiary as well. State officials, including governors, would visit our home for dinner. As someone with an innate sense of public relations, Dad courted legislators with lunches and dinners because he was subject to their mercy for the prison budgets.

Dad also maintained an open-door policy with the press.

Reporters could come and talk to any inmate at any time that they wanted. There was no suppression of any kind. The same applied for state officials and legislators. Dad was straightforward, honest and gained a wealth of respect among the community. Despite the flip of the governorship between Democrat and Republican, he would keep his position throughout the years.

Jerry, Pat, and Lou in Mullen, Idaho. (Courtesy of the Clapp Family)

Lou Clapp. (Courtesy of the Clapp Family)

Margaret "Robb" Robbins at the Stibnite Post Office. (Courtesy of the Clapp Family)

Jerry in 1936. (Courtesy of the Clapp Family)

Robb and Lou Clapp. (Courtesy of the Clapp Family)

Lou Clapp (left) with fellow officers in Wallace, Idaho. (Courtesy of the Clapp Family)

Young Jerry had plenty of space to play. (Courtesy of the Clapp Family)

Chapter 3

Growing up Tough

Before moving to the penitentiary, my childhood was perfectly normal. I played with the other kids living in our northern Idaho town. Because it was a small town with very few age-appropriate activities for kids to engage in, we had to find our own forms of entertainment. Of course, at the time, I didn't realize Wallace was an infamous red-light district; that fact became known to me after I enrolled at the University of Idaho in Moscow many years later.

Outside of school, we took advantage of the natural landscape and rode our bikes around town. The local candy store was a central meeting place before a trek into the nearby forest. Summers were warm, so children often played in the streams or climbed trees. Winters saw deep snow, but the hills were perfect for sledding. After rushing home from school to grab our sleds, we would seek out the best spot to build the fastest track.

Most of my friends were children of miners who worked to find silver in the surrounding mountains. Since their fathers were usually strong and hard-working men, many of their sons were rough. It was a very macho society and the toughest kids got a lot of attention. At school, the local boys always had four or five fights going on. We did it for entertainment. During the lunch hour and recess, we would gather on the playgrounds to watch the fights of the day. At the beginning of recess, boys would break away from the girls and start tussling. You could walk from one fight to another or get in one yourself. That was always quite easy, and that was how you built your reputation. We abided by our interpretation of the Marquess of Queensbury rules established in British boxing. Girls often watched us fight from afar. They would either look on with unimpressed indifference or wait nearby for the fight to end, grooming themselves in hope that we would notice them. At least that's how it seemed to us boys. As I remember, the girls who were most anxious for attention rarely got it because our fights were only broken up by the ringing of the school bell.

Growing up with my dad being a law enforcement officer wasn't hard, by any means. But I never got away with anything! Everyone in town knew me, and knew my dad, and word of my activities traveled fast. It was particularly difficult to go unnoticed when we lived in Wallace. The small town did not lend itself to privacy. You would think people would be too busy with everything else going on in the town to focus on what a young boy did in his spare time. I never intentionally misbehaved or got into trouble, but somehow, I would end up being quizzed by my dad at the dinner table.

"Anything you want to tell me tonight, Jerry?" Dad would ask.

He did this specifically when he already knew I did, in fact, have something to tell him. Plus, he already knew the answer. I never lied to my dad; he was honest with me and expected the same.

"Jerry, I will understand anything you ever do so long as you tell me the truth."

Dad felt strongly about honesty. When I did things wrong, as all children do, he would never punish me so long as I confessed to any wrongdoing.

With so many eyes on me in Wallace, it came as no surprise whenever Dad asked me that fateful question. On one such occasion, I admitted to sneaking into his closet and finding a box full of silver dollars. I had never seen them before and figured a single piece wouldn't be missed. So, I took a silver dollar, gathered my friends, and headed off to the local candy shop. We selected all our favorite candy and I, the one with the money, was the hero of the group. I confidently paid with my silver dollar and we made our way to the communal climbing tree to relish in our haul.

"I heard about your candy shop purchase," Dad said calmly. "The owner called to inform me that you were using counterfeit money to buy treats for your friends."

I remember gathering my thoughts, looking for an honest way out of this mess. *Counterfeit money?*

"Dad, I didn't mean to buy candy with fake money. I didn't realize it wasn't real."

Because I had been forthcoming with the transgression, Dad let it slide under one stipulation, I had to pay the candy shop owner back for all the candy that my friends and I had consumed.

Later that evening, I couldn't help but ask. "Dad, how did the candy shop man know it was counterfeit?"

"When you put the money on the glass countertop, the dollar didn't clink," he said. "Instead, the owner heard it clunk." With this, he took a silver dollar from each pocket. "This one is real, and this one was from the box in my closet, a place where you are not supposed to be."

I nodded, certainly looking remorseful.

The two coins looked identical, but each made a different tone when they hit the table.

At that point, I felt it only fair to ask Dad why he had so much counterfeit money in the closet. To be honest, I don't remember the answer, but I assume it was evidence from some crime he had solved.

Jerry in northern Idaho. (Courtesy of the Clapp Family)

Chapter 4

New Kid on the Block

As I mentioned, Dad and I arrived at the prison in January of 1945. My mother, Margaret (better known as Robb) and my younger sister, Pat, stayed in northern Idaho to sell the house and tie up loose ends before joining us in Boise. Until they arrived with more furniture, our new home was sparsely decorated. For the first several months, it was just dad and me living there. We had our houseboys and cooks, but they left at the end of every shift, leaving us alone. Despite being surrounded by a small population of people, the house felt quiet and lonely before my mother and sister arrived.

When Dad had announced that we were moving to Boise, I bid farewell to all my friends in Wallace. I would miss them but knew I would be able to make new friends. How different could life in Boise be than Wallace? Turns out, it was completely dissimilar to growing up in a rural mining town.

My new classmates at Roosevelt Elementary School were city kids. Compared to them, I was sort of rough and hardened for a 10-year-old. I was skinny and taller than most of them, but being the new kid, I was naturally subject to bullying at first. I lived at the prison and my father assigned guards to drive me around. The other kids would tease me when I walked from the school to the prison vehicle. After a week of this treatment, I had had enough and decided to settle it the only way I knew how. Twice, on the way to the car, I started fights with my tormentors. I won them both.

28

I became accustomed to my new school life quickly and thought Boise was a pretty mild town. At school, even though I missed my old boxing friends, I refrained from my urge to fight the other boys. At the same time, Roosevelt was structured, and I felt well-regimented there. I was a good student in grammar school. It wasn't easy for me, but the teachers liked me, and I stayed out of trouble.

I had always enjoyed reading, but it became a staple to my personal entertainment after we moved to Boise. When I was in grammar school up north, I would read books such as *Treasure Island.* My school friends and I would talk about them; we would pretend to be swashbuckling pirates when we weren't fighting.

When we first came to the prison, Dad was reluctant for me to bring friends home. Once Mom and my sister moved to Boise, I was occasionally allowed to invite friends home from school or to play on weekends. But those times were few, probably because of the liability. Maybe Dad was concerned an inmate might grab one of my friends as a hostage. Even though he stayed on high alert, Dad didn't want to expose innocent people to possible danger. He was always concerned about the wellbeing of my friends. Also, we were at least a mile outside the city limits and there weren't any families living close. Parents were unlikely to drive their kids to the prison, let alone leave them. I can only imagine how my friends' parents felt knowing their child was out playing near so many criminals.

Despite all of this, when I did bring any friends out to the prison, they would always be more than anxious and intrigued. To be safe, I would go through the same steps as any other day. My friend and I would inform the turnkey of our destination and then proceed to explore the grounds. Our favorite places to explore were the rock house a short distance from the prison. We would also hike up Table Rock on nice days. Sometimes we packed sandwiches and stayed up there for a while, watching the inmates from above. After those outings, we would be hot and tired, so we would exchange a bit of money for the plastic coins accepted in the prison commissary and buy a soda. While I was accustomed to purchasing soda at the commissary, the novelty of it never seemed to wear off for my friends.

Jerry and Pal. (Courtesy of the Clapp Family)

Robb and Pal. (Courtesy of the Clapp Family)

Chapter 5

An Overwhelming World

When I first saw the prison, it looked like something out of the old west. Opened in 1872, it featured 17-foot walls and guard towers made of sandstone. Inside were several buildings with various levels of cells, housing about 500 inmates at any given time. Most of the cells were tight and sparse. Depending on the crime and attitude, some prisoners had nicer accommodations, but nobody was incarcerated in luxury.

Our house was located about 100 feet from the northwestern wall of the large men's prison, my bedroom window with a direct view of the penitentiary.

Up the road, to the north of the administration building, was a smaller women's ward of the prison. It was basically a cellblock with a yard and sandstone walls.

Idaho State Penitentiary, circa 1945. (Idaho State Archives)

Chapter 6

The Quiet Blacksmith

At the beginning of our time in Boise, Dad and I toured the prison with staff members who knew the ins and outs of penitentiary life. Since I could not be left alone in the house, there was no other option but for me to tag along. I stayed close to my father the whole time as he surveyed these new stomping grounds. During the exploration, Dad and I were introduced to all the guards, many of the prisoners and trusties.

Trusties were low-security inmates who could be trusted to be on their best behavior. They performed essential prison tasks and were able to wander around the grounds completing their work. Some were even allowed to work outside the heavy iron gates. They were given this measure of comfort as long as they performed their tasks and abided by the rules . . . as long as they didn't leave.

One of the first trusties we met was the prison blacksmith, a man
named Abraham Rich. He was stationed in a large workshop just outside the wall, but on the very far side of the prison. In his mid-fifties, he was a smug-looking man with short grey hair and a mouth that was always a little turned down on both sides.

Dad spoke with Rich about his responsibilities. Rich talked about how he primarily maintained the horses and their shoes, but his favorite task was knife making. He showed us various knives he had constructed from available metal. *A prisoner who gets to make knives?* I nervously scooted behind my dad, trying not to be noticed.

Seemingly unphased, my father continued speaking to the inmate. Rich was very frank in his responses.

"I'm a lone wolf, Warden," he said. "I don't have much use for the other inmates or anybody else for that matter. I prefer to be out here in my shop alone. I get more work done."

After leaving the blacksmith's shop, my dad asked the Deputy Warden with us more about Rich. Dad was curious about how long Rich had been there, whether he caused any trouble as a prisoner and what his crime had been. The Deputy Warden obliged, answering all the questions.

"He's in for incest, Warden."

At the time, being only 10 years old, I didn't understand the disgusted expression on my dad's face. As an adult, I thought back on that moment and many more related to Rich with discomfort.

Exactly two months after we met the blacksmith, he escaped. On March 8, 1945, Rich saw an opportunity and took it. Having been assigned to go check the horses' shoes at Eagle Island Farm, Rich rode in the bus to the farm and went to work in the stables. No one was sure how it happened, but a guard turned his back for just a moment and when he checked again, the convict was gone. Rich managed to walk away from the farm without detection in broad daylight. A typical manhunt ensued; guards and law enforcement persons searched the surrounding area. Unfortunately, he had disappeared completely.

Prison staff were stunned that Rich would take such a risk; he was up for parole the next month, April of 1945. If he had been caught, he would have been kept in the prison longer, his trusty status revoked and not given the chance to apply for parole.

A month after the search was called off, the State Pardon Board received an unusual application. It was from Rich, seeking his pardon. Aware that he had just escaped, the authorities denied his application. However, there was always a mystery surrounding the application. No one could figure out how Rich filed it undetected. Abraham Rich was never seen again by law enforcement. In all his years as warden, my dad would catch all the men who tried to escape . . . except Rich.

Chapter 7

Serious Boundaries

Dad was the youngest warden the state had ever seen, so the prison guards were not used to having children wandering independently around the penitentiary grounds. They all took it in stride and made every effort to protect my sister and me from the criminals locked up inside the sandstone walls.

Living at the penitentiary, I followed Dad's rules. I always understood the danger I could be in if I put one foot out of line. I was free to wander inside the walls and the surrounding foothills, but I was always required to inform the prison turnkey if I was leaving the front yard of our family home. I would make my way to the main gate that led to the prison yard, passing dad's office. The turnkey usually on duty when I was heading out to play was a man named Merritt Lavender. As with many of the guards and prison employees, I spent time getting to know Lavender. He told me about his former job with the Lewiston Police Department, being hired as a prison guard, and promoted to turnkey. Having the responsibility of being the final defense of the prison walls, he boasted about knowing all the movements and comings and goings within the prison. His job required it.

"Where are you heading today, Jerry?"

I would tell him where I was going.

"Let me radio the tower guards so they know to keep an eye out for you."

I would wait while he spoke into his radio and get a fuzzy, hard to distinguish confirmation from the tower guards.

"You have fun out there," Lavender would say as I trotted off, waving back to him, excited for whatever the day might hold in store for me.

It wasn't until I was much older and thought back on my experiences as a child that I truly gave Lavender the credit he deserved. I probably owe my life to that man because he knew my every move throughout my many adventures within the prison.

I was incredibly lucky to have the freedom I did. The latitude I was given did not translate to my younger sister's experience at the prison. Pat had a much shorter leash. Pat's restrictions involved never being alone outside of the house. And she wasn't. When she went to school, at St. Teresa's Academy, there was a guard. When she came home, there was a guard. Pat was driven everywhere she needed to go either by our parents or a prison staff member. Even when Pat became a teenager, she would be confined to the front yard. Although she never seemed to question it, even her boyfriend would have a hard time getting through the gate to see her.

Pat was very young when she and our mother arrived at the prison. One day, she left the front yard with the dog and began walking toward the Administration Building, possibly to visit Dad. Chief Deputy Warden Paris "Pat" O'Neil saw her small frame in the walkway. He quickly went up to my sister and told her to go back to the front yard where our mother could see her. Because she was young, unaware of the potential danger and just a touch defiant, she turned her head towards O'Neil and said, "No!"

The tough-talking, tobacco-chewing man had a soft side when it came to my sister and me.

"You know it's real important you stay in the yard," he said. "It's safe there."

Pat stood her ground.

O'Neil sighed at my sister and bent down to pick up a stick. Pal immediately perked up in excitement.

"Now, you take Pal and stay in the yard," O'Neil grunted as he chucked the stick onto our front lawn. Both ran back to our yard.

Regardless of our highly protected upbringing, Pat and I attempted to be normal kids. I eventually felt very relaxed around the prison; I was even allowed to visit Harry Orchard—one of the most notorious criminals in Idaho history—on the poultry ranch by myself. When I got a little bit older, I had full access to the trusties' quarters and could enter the walls of the prison without a guard escorting me to the barber. One guard kept a particularly watchful eye over me when I would travel to the prison farms with the Bull Gang; a group of inmates who were taken out of the prison walls by truck to work either on the Mosley or the Eagle Island prison farms.

Even though I had more boundaries than most children, my parents made every effort for me to grow up like any other young man in Boise at the time. They worked hard to give Pat and I a normal childhood. They did not stifle our unique personalities and gave us the freedom to be who we wanted.

Still, my childhood and young adult life could not compare to anyone else's. And even though I was given liberties, it was still a strict upbringing in the sense that I had to comply with any rules my dad put forth, not just for his peace of mind, but for my own safety. I was old enough when we moved to the prison to understand this and I never questioned it. Even so, I often pushed the boundaries, whether intentional or not.

I liked to have fun with my friends and there were times we mindlessly messed around. It was usually me that caused the most trouble, though, and I didn't always think through the consequences. I had a knack for mischief.

I think we functioned like most families at the time. We took short vacations to the McCall area, my parents had an active social life away from the prison, Dad hosted poker nights in the basement of our home, and my sister often competed in swimming events. Living at the prison did not put a blanket over our lives; it merely placed tighter restrictions on our activities. We had to leave the phone number of where we were always going to be. Even when we were not physically at the penitentiary, someone was keeping tabs on us. To me, that was perfectly normal.

Jerry, Pat, and their grandmothers. (Courtesy of the Clapp Family)

Pat and her father in front of the Warden's House. (Courtesy of the Clapp Family)

Chapter 8

Trusties in the Home

There were, of course, varying levels of security at the penitentiary, so I primarily spent my time getting to know those inmates who were not confined to solitary or the maximum-security areas— particularly trusties. They may have been prisoners, but they were also my neighbors and I got to know them as such, even forming some personal relationships. Funny, I can remember their nicknames more than their real names, although not every trusty who I interacted with had an impact on me.

There were pump house attendants and poultry farmers. I'd go up to the blacksmith shop to watch the work. I was even shown by a trusty how they would slaughter the cattle.

One position always held by a trusty was that of the warden's resident house boy or girl. They handled most of the general domestic duties around the house. They would clean, do laundry, do the ironing, and help the cook with cleaning the dishes. Occasionally, they were even required to mind my sister and me. Because these trusties spent so much time in our home, I got to know several of them quite well.

Chris Kristiansen (right) and James Turner Owens at the Warden's House in 1946.
(Courtesy of the Clapp Family)

43

Chapter 9

The Beautiful Arlene

When Dad and I first arrived at the penitentiary, we readied our new home as best we could before Mom arrived with Pat. We did not have much by way of furniture, so it wasn't difficult to get things moved in. However, the cooking and cleaning aspect stumped us. I'm not entirely sure if previous wardens had employed the female or male inmates, but Dad decided to give two female prisoners the roles of cook and house girl. I expect he selected women to run the household because that seemed natural to him; my mother and grandmother had always done the cooking and cleaning. Perhaps my dad thought women would have a better influence on me at that age than two male prisoners.

I was excited the day the women's ward inmates were due to start their jobs in our home. My dad had met and spoken to them before that morning, wanting to make sure we would all get along. And I had seen one of them from a distance. I don't recall much of anything about the cook. She was just another old woman as far as I was concerned. On the other hand, the inmate appointed to be our house girl was young, just barely 18, if I remember correctly. Her name was Arlene Dagget McWilliams and she was very pretty, even without being dolled up like she was in her booking photo. Even though I was shy around girls, she struck my fancy.

"Jerry, come down here," Dad called up the stairs. I had been combing my hair, making sure it looked neat for our new staff.

44

"Coming, Dad. Be right down."

Satisfied that I would make a good first impression on Arlene, I trotted down the hall and practically ran down the stairs. Misjudging the steps, I tripped on something (possibly my own feet) and tumbled down. *So much for my hair being nicely combed*, I thought as I scrambled up from the floor.

I looked cautiously at Arlene; she was giggling. Dad introduced the two women and I nodded by way of greeting them. The women went about their duties while I followed Arlene around the house, undoubtedly being a pest to the attractive young woman.

For the next week or so, Arlene would let me hang around while she did her cleaning. In that time, she told me more about herself. Until then, I'd never heard of a place called St. Anthony's Juvenile Reformatory, but Arlene had spent two years there. She had committed a few robberies and got caught at the age of twelve. After she left St. Anthony's, she got married.

Awfully young to be married, I thought, but listened intently regardless. Arlene explained that the marriage ended because her husband got convicted for robbery not long after the wedding. Once he was in jail, she divorced him and married another man named Verdelle McWilliams, who was now serving time in the men's portion of our penitentiary. Arlene liked bad boys.

"I met Verdelle in Texas after he was paroled from prison there," Arlene told me. "After we got married, we moved to Washington. Verdelle and I needed money, so he got a job at a shipyard in Vancouver." Arlene proceeded to tell me about Verdelle's request for a $30 advance on his paycheck. That was a decent amount of money in 1944. Arlene told me they used that money to fund their honeymoon around the Pacific Northwest. I believed her.

"We took a nice little trip to Portland and then decided to drive around northern Idaho for a bit." She boasted about the items she received as "wedding gifts" throughout their Pacific Northwest honeymoon.

"My favorites were the two fur coats I got from the department store," Arlene sighed, looking into the distance with a wistful look on her face. "Oh, and the jewelry was so glamorous."

Because I didn't know any better, I honestly thought she was talking about gifts she had received.

Arlene was talkative. I believed she must have been glamorous enough to wear fur coats and lots of jewelry before being booked; her photo was enough evidence of that. Her style had been tamed by prison life, but I saw her pinching her cheeks throughout the day to make them appear rouged. I liked her personality, as well as her appearance. She was vivacious and, despite being an inmate in the state prison, had a lot of charisma. I was charmed by her fun spirit, liking her more and more each day she worked in the house.

One day, I came down the stairs to the kitchen to find a male inmate serving breakfast. I asked if Arlene was still coming in to clean and do the laundry that day. My dad, who was drinking coffee, told me she had been reassigned to another job. *What? That can't be.* I was put out, sulking all day about the new houseboy on duty. I didn't understand at the time why my dad had reassigned Arlene. *She was doing a fine job!* Apparently, Dad had noticed how taken I was by the young woman and decided that Arlene could be a bad influence on me. Being in my formative years and impressionable around a beautiful female inmate, I suppose it might have been a bad idea in the long run. However, at the time, I was sad to see Arlene go.

Later in life, I would ask my dad about Arlene. He informed me that her "honeymoon" with Verdelle had been a prolonged heist through three different states. According to Dad, the young woman and her new husband took the advanced paycheck money and left Vancouver. When they arrived in Portland, Verdelle and Arlene robbed a series of businesses including a café, two gas stations, and a cleaner. They even broke into an apartment and took whatever they could find of value. When they felt their presence in Portland might be noticed, they went north and returned to Vancouver, where Verdelle got his hands on an automatic pistol and they held up a department store (Arlene's beloved fur coats) and several jewelry stores (her fondness for sparkly items).

Dad continued to tell the saga of Arlene and Verdelle. He knew it well because Arlene's file contained a 40-page confession. Apparently, Arlene had been given a shorter sentence in exchange for information about Verdelle's part in their series of crimes. Amazed that a confession could be so long, I listened intently. Dad told me the couple tried getting a room in a fully booked hotel. Instead of turning them away, the manager allowed them to sleep in the lobby. Sometime in the middle of the night, Verdelle snuck behind the hotel desk and emptied the cashbox before leaving the hotel for Coeur d'Alene. Arlene's confession detailed that their heists in the northern Idaho town also included a radio store, barbershop, and an oil station. Before leaving Coeur d'Alene, the two thieves sold their stash of jewelry and used the money to purchase a car. The same day they bought the car, they returned to the dealership. According to them, the gearshift wasn't functioning correctly. The mechanic told the couple no one else was in the office, but to go ahead and wait while he checked the vehicle. While the mechanic was distracted, the Honeymooners emptied the cashbox, taking back all the money they used to buy the car.

At this point in Dad's retelling of Arlene's very long confession, he chuckled and told me authorities had been trailing the couple the entire time. Investigators had observed Arlene and Verdelle throughout their 15 crimes in Washington, Oregon and Idaho. After leaving the car dealership, police apprehended and arrested the young couple. With evidence stacked against them, Arlene accepted an agreement from the prosecutors to implicate Verdelle and receive a lighter sentence. Ultimately, Arlene only served 11 months before being paroled. As far as I can recall, she was the only female inmate I found attractive.

Arlene McWilliams (left) with an inmate identified as Dorothy outside the Women's Ward. (Courtesy of the Clapp Family)

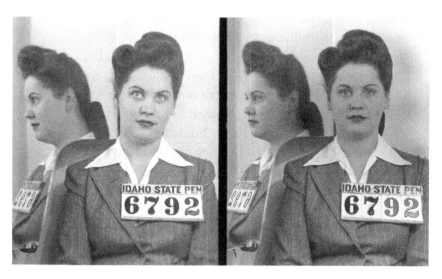

Arlene Dagget McWilliams Booking Photo. (Idaho State Archives)

Chapter 10

Prisoner and Role Model

Originally from Brooklyn, New York, Clarence "Chris" Kristiansen had served as a Lieutenant in the Army for seven years at the time of his conviction. Prior to being stationed as second-in-command at the Prisoner of War Camp in Marsing, Idaho, Kristiansen had been decorated during World War II with a Silver Star, a Bronze Star, a Purple Heart and four battle stars. These were awarded to him for his bravery during combat in Africa, Italy, France and Germany.

On Friday night, July 27, 1945, Kristiansen was returning to the POW camp after an evening out on the town. Driving a half-ton Army truck and admittedly intoxicated, Kristiansen was heading south of Caldwell, through the farming area of Sunnyslope, making his way to Marsing. It was 9:30 p.m., so the summer light was darkening fast when Kristiansen collided with a group of children horseback riding along Highway 55. Despite the impact, Kristiansen continued driving, fleeing the scene. Unfortunately, this horrible accident caused fatal injuries to a young girl named Carolyn Ann Symms. She was just eight years old. The horse she had been riding, as well as one of the other horses, also perished due to Kristiansen's drunk driving.

Kristiansen pled guilty and was convicted of involuntary manslaughter, booked into the prison in October of '45 with a sentence of six months to ten years. He was 25 years old, remorseful that he had done something so terribly wrong and willing to pay the price.

Because he was not a re-offending or blatantly dangerous criminal, Kristiansen was rather quickly made a trusty. The young man had a good head on his shoulders and my father liked him quite a lot. Dad also trusted him more than other inmates, probably due to his excellent moral conduct. Almost immediately upon his arrival, Kristiansen was appointed by Dad as one of our houseboys.

In the 10 months of his incarceration, I developed a close friendship with Kristiansen. A few times, in a brotherly fashion, he would carry me around the prison grounds on his shoulders. My dad felt comfortable letting me roam about as long as Kristiansen was with me. He practically became part of the family.

Kristiansen was so well-liked by my dad that, in the summer of 1946, he was invited on our family vacation to Cox's Dude Ranch in Yellow Pine. There, Kristiansen and I rode horses, fished, and watched as salmon came up Johnson Creek to spawn.

Not only was Kristiansen an accomplished outdoorsman, he was also a gifted storyteller and artist. I was fascinated with stories of his experiences in World War II and the cultures he had encountered in Africa and Europe. He often described life in Brooklyn before joining the Army and how excited he was to return home to see his family after such a long time away. Being an avid reader, Kristiansen introduced me to writers such as Omar Khayyam, of whom I became a big fan. On top of his impressive love of ancient literature and overall knowledge of the world, Kristiansen was talented with a paint brush. He would make lapel pins and paint cougars or pheasants on them; his attention to detail was stunning. To make a little extra money with his release from prison on the horizon, Kristiansen sold these lapel pins to guards and prison visitors. Being as patient as he was with me, he taught me how to paint and draw wildlife, usually on a larger scale.

Kristiansen filed for clemency several times in the first six months of his incarceration. The Governor and Attorney General of Idaho at the time both considered his outstanding military career before giving him a full pardon. Kristiansen's prison sentence ended on August 1, 1946 and his reputation of being a reliable and respectable member of society was restored, despite a group of protestors from Marsing. At the time, I just thought they were attempting to drag his name through the mud, although now I realize their pain and anger about what he had done.

He left Idaho for a city on the East Coast where he became the president of a company. In the little correspondence we had after he left Boise, Kristiansen informed us that he had married a young woman from Pennsylvania; she was a teacher.

Because I was 11 years old when I first met Kristiansen, I felt a brotherly bond with him. Unlike my other friendships with inmates as a pre-teen and teen, the closeness I felt to Kristiansen stayed with me for my entire life. He taught me about foreign cultures and history. I trusted him and looked up to him, hoping I could be as smart and talented as him. Kristiansen served his sentence with dignity and composure. He then dedicated himself to being a successful and upstanding citizen.

My days with Kristiansen were some of the best in my memory of growing up at the penitentiary. He influenced my life and my tribute to him was naming my eldest son Chris.

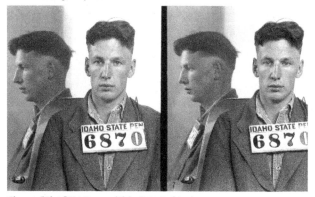

Clarence "Chris" Kristiansen. (Idaho State Archives)

Lou (left), unidentified friend, Jerry, and Chris Kristiansen during 1946 fishing trip in Yellow Pine. (Courtesy of the Clapp Family)

At 12, Jerry was already an expert fisherman. (Courtesy of the Clapp Family)

Chapter 11

You Can't Always Trust a Convicted Killer

J. Britt Hargraves, Jr. had killed a deputy marshal who was called to a family dispute near Pocatello, then wounded two more law officers during his arrest. He had been given a death sentence which was commuted to life in prison.

Despite his crime, Hargraves was considered a well-behaved inmate and reached trusty status when my dad was warden. He was given a relatively solitary work assignment, managing the hot water plant, which was located across the field from our house, away from the prison.

One night, my family was having dinner when Chief Deputy Warden O'Neil knocked on our door. O'Neil informed my dad that he and the guards had solid evidence that Hargraves was leaving the hot water plant and venturing into the main downtown area of Boise. Understandably agitated, my dad told me to go with him and O'Neil. The three of us got into the Chief Deputy Warden's vehicle and drove to the hot water plant to investigate, figuring we would then head downtown.

Upon arriving at the hot water plant, my dad opened the door only to find Hargraves standing there. He smelled strongly of alcohol.

"Britt, we understand you've been leaving to go downtown," Dad said. "We need to put you back in the yard."

Hargraves nodded and seemingly accepted this announcement.

"I knew you would catch me eventually, Warden," he said with a sigh. "I've got some personal items in the box across the room. Do you permit me to gather them before we leave?"

My dad allowed it. But as Hargraves started moving toward the box, O'Neil shouted, "Britt, STOP!"

The inmate froze. After my dad had a solid grip on Hargraves, the Chief Deputy Warden opened the box and lifted the towel that could be seen inside. Resting there was a loaded .38 revolver. Rather surprised and shaken by this development, my dad escorted Hargraves back to the prison yard while O'Neil handled the weapon.

We had to agree that the Chief Deputy Warden had saved our lives that night. Without definitive proof, my young mind firmly believed that Hargraves would have killed the three of us with the loaded gun and escaped in our vehicle.

After spending a lot of time confined to the yard, Hargraves managed to work his way up to trusty status again. However, his new assignment was commissary attendant. Although he was no longer able to wander off the prison grounds, he still had a coveted role, and was responsible for a lot of inventory. This included candy, sodas, and the most demanded item in the prison: cigarettes. Hargraves was also trusted with the money used to complete commissary transactions; money that came from both inmates and guards. Hargraves never attempted to escape again.

J. Britt Hargraves. (Idaho State Archives)

Chapter 12

The Creepy Twin Sisters

Until I was well into my teens, I had no interest in girls. There were a few occasions—like being around Arlene McWilliams—when I felt myself blush in the presence of a pretty woman, but girls my own age were at the bottom of my priority list. As far as I was concerned, all they did was sit around playing with dolls or fidgeting with their dresses and bows. I didn't have time for that kind of silliness in my busy schedule. Spending time with my little sister was more than enough when it came to girls.

Luckily, none of my school friends were interested in girls at that point either. The boys I played with at school liked to ride bikes and wander in the foothills. We were all certain girls were from a different planet.

Occasionally, Bob Hawon "Big Bob" Stubblefield and his family would come over for dinner. Big Bob was one of my favorite guards, except for one thing—the Stubblefield's had adopted twin daughters, Mary Ann and Eva May. They were about my age and it somehow became my duty to entertain them while our parents socialized. Every time, it was torture. I couldn't stand them.

When we were about 12, Mary Ann and Eva May found their way to my room even though I had gone there to seek solitude from their annoying giggling. Knowing I would get into trouble if I was rude to our guests, I made a valiant attempt to show Mary Ann and Eva May the model airplane I was putting together. Mary Ann sat on the edge of my bed, completely unenthused by the project sprawled out on my desk. Eva May stood awkwardly close to me while I demonstrated how the propeller spun on the nose of the model plane. She was nodding and staring at me intently. I began to inch away, trying to stay as far away from the girl as politely possible. Suddenly, she reached out and grabbed my hand. My face started to feel hot.

"Jerry Clapp." Eva May's bossy tone split through the room. "I want you to kiss me. Right now."

I froze, my face growing hotter by the second. I shook my head, unable to speak. Scared to look away from Eva May, I hoped her sister might step in. Mary Ann was paying no attention to the scene unfolding in front of her.

"Come on," Eva May demanded, bending a little at the hip, leaning close to my face. "Kiss me on the lips." She closed her eyes and pursed her lips expectantly.

Beginning to panic that she was coming in for the kiss, I clenched my lips tightly together and pulled my hand away from hers. Her hand was very sweaty, so escaping her grasp was surprisingly easy. Fortunately, just as I was trying to figure out what to do next, their father's voice boomed from the bottom of the stairs.

"Let's go, girls. Mother has dinner waiting for us by now."

Mary Ann hopped off the bed and stepped toward the door.

"Bye, Jerry. See you at school."

I waved my farewell to the girl and motioned toward the open bedroom for Eva May to follow her twin. Eva May let out a displeased hmph and left. I could hear her saddle shoes stomping deliberately down the stairs. I let out a sigh of relief, grateful to have narrowly avoided being kissed. I went to the bathroom down the hall and put cold water on my face to make the blushing stop. After that, I tried to avoid the Stubblefield sisters for a long time.

Mary Ann and Eva May Stubblefield (Row 2, second and third from left) in a yearbook photo. (Ancestry.com)

Chapter 13

Big Bob and the Bull Gang of Eagle Island

A lot of the escapes were orchestrated from the Eagle Island Honor Farm. Functioning since 1929, the farm had been home to one hundred trusties at any given time. Naturally, some of those men would get itchy feet and try to escape. They rarely succeeded. Locals of Eagle would see the inmates in town, their pants soaked from walking through the Boise river, and call the farm superintendent.

"Big Bob" Stubblefield was promoted by my dad within a year of them working together. Stubblefield was good with inmates and had the skills to manage them outside of the walls. Big and intimidating, he had the perfect traits for a guard and Bull Gang manager.

Having been a deputy sheriff in Grangeville prior to becoming a guard at the state pen, Stubblefield had a similar background to my dad, which they bonded over. Born in 1878, Stubblefield moved from Arkansas to Idaho as a young child. Because of his size and strength, he worked in the mining and timber industries before becoming a deputy sheriff in 1925. Stubblefield began working at the prison in 1936, stationed as a guard before his promotion to oversee the Bull Gang.

My parents felt comfortable leaving me in Stubblefield's care when we drove to the prison farms. I was free to travel with Big Bob and the Bull Gang whenever I wanted with the condition that I stayed close to him. My dad knew that no inmate would ever touch me with Stubblefield nearby.

The truck, loaded with trusties, would pick me up at my house. I would get in front with Stubblefield and an inmate driver. We would go to one of the prison farms where we would watch the inmates work. At the end of the day, the Bull Gang would be taken back to the prison. I always looked forward to those rides.

Stubblefield would tell me stories about his life prior to working at the prison. According to one story he told me, Stubblefield had once had to hit a man at a bar in Idaho City. The blow had knocked the man through a wall so hard they thought he was dead. Inmates have a way of finding out about the backgrounds of prison staff. Nobody ever escaped from Big Bob. There was no way they wanted to mess with him, even if he was almost 70 years old.

"Big Bob" Stubblefield. (Idaho State Archives)

Chapter 14

A Tree Grows in the Women's Ward

The women's ward of the Idaho State Penitentiary was usually much quieter than the men's area of the prison. First, it housed fewer inmates. Also, the women were generally better behaved than the men.

While still under Dad's watchful eye, the ward was run by a matron for a few hours every morning, leaving the female prison population unattended for the afternoons and evenings. There were no guards at night either. Because it was located close to the guard's quarters and administrative office, the women's prison was considered to have enough surveillance.

Outside of their cell block, the women inmates had a large yard where they could exercise, relax, and often sunbathe. At one time, there also was a large tree in the middle of the yard.

It was a warm summer evening; the sun was beginning to creep towards the horizon, the foothills were glowing orange, reflecting the sunset. The prison had been peaceful for what seemed like a record length of time. After our family dinner, we were on the porch enjoying the weather. A light breeze from the north carried the sound of voices to our ears. The voices were those of men, hooting and hollering, cheering for something.

Dad wandered to the edge of our yard to get a slightly closer look at the situation causing the commotion. I went to stand next to him, curious to see what could be so exciting. In the distance, peeking over the top of the women's ward wall, was a large tree. The green leaves thick and healthy. In the tree were two women, supported by strong branches. The women didn't seem to be making any attempt toward escape. Rather, they were entertaining the men who gathered, just on the other side of the wall that separated the women's yard from the trusties' area of the prison grounds. The two women were performing strip-tease dances in the branches, much to the pleasure of the guards and trusties who were cheering them on. I could hear my dad swearing under his breath. This wasn't the first time this had happened in that tree.

"Come on, Jerry," Dad muttered. "Let's take care of this situation."

He led me out of the yard and to his car. By the time we drove up to the women's ward there were no guards or trusties to be seen. The women in the tree had also disappeared. They all must have heard Dad's car driving up the gravel road. My dad parked his car and we walked into the trusties' quarters, Dad requesting that two men come with us. Once the two trusties were in the car with us, we drove up the road to one of the nearby prison farms. There, my dad opened a door to one of the barns and removed a chainsaw, putting it in the back end of the vehicle. The four of us returned to the women's prison. Chainsaw in tow, my dad used his key to enter and we marched around the building to the yard where Dad instructed the two trusties to cut down the tree. Once it was on the ground, Dad told them to cut the tree into pieces small enough for a residential fireplace.

As the tree was being completely chopped, dismantled, and hauled off to the warden's residence by the trusties, Dad talked with the women in the center of the ward.

"I don't suppose anyone would like to tell me who was doing the striptease up in the tree?"

No one said anything. He told them the fate of the tree, as if the sound of the chainsaw outside wasn't enough indication that their tree was gone. By the time all but a few pieces of kindling were left in the women's ward yard, it was late. The sun had set; the foothills were a deep shade of black against a dark blue sky.

The women's ward was quiet for the rest of the night. The prison grounds peaceful and somber. Nothing more happened until the next morning. Upon entering his office, Dad found a note on his desk. The bit of writing said "Warden, Warden, spare that tree. In life it has sheltered me." The note was based on an old song which had started with the phrase "woodman, woodman, spare that tree" by George Pope Morris. Dad could only assume the matron had brought the note in from an inmate of the women's ward. The tree was gone; it was too late to spare it.

However, the lack of a tree in their yard did not deter the women from continuing to perform strip-tease dances.

East Wing of the Women's Ward. (Idaho State Archives)

Chapter 15

The Art of Sensing a Riot

Riots break out all the time in prisons. It comes with the territory. But not on my dad's watch. Yes, there were times when restlessness got the better of some inmates and a sense of unease was in the air. There were horrible beatings and attacks, too. But as far as prison-wide riots, during the 21 years Dad was warden of the Idaho State Penitentiary, only two riots occurred.

"There isn't a prison in the world that doesn't have the possibility of such riots," Dad always said. "But we must maintain discipline."

It is easy to understand why he was so cautious when inmates started becoming agitated. There were a lot of innocent people in the near vicinity— primarily his own wife and children—who could be used against him if things went south.

There could have been more riots if Dad had not ended them before they began. He could just feel it; the unrest that came with certain seasons. He used to say, "I started every riot that happened in this prison." He used to start them at 9 am in broad daylight. When a riot occurs at night you don't have control, you can't tell where people are, or what they are doing. He would have already alerted the state police and other law enforcement so he would have plenty of back up. He usually knew who the ringleaders were from informants; trusties from the yard who would provide details ahead of time, or guards who would hear mutterings between inmates. Dad would order the guards to lock up the ringleaders in Siberia, and that would normally trigger the riot.

Once, the inmates were planning a full-blown riot because of the quality of food being served in the cafeteria. Keep in mind that inmates cooked the food and almost all of it was sourced from the prison farms. The "gruel" they were required to cook for themselves was made with fresh or home preserved ingredients. But in the spring before new crops were harvested, the prisoners were still thawing out from the winter blues.

When the rumor of a calculated riot reached my dad, he jumped into action before the whole prison population was in uproar. He spoke with several of the leaders in this proposed uprising, asking to hear their concerns and demands.

"Warden, all we want is a few good meals," they told him. "The slop we have in the cafeteria is horrible."

Dad listened and considered their request.

"I'll tell you what," he said in his tough but fair way. "The cook I have at my house right now is quite good. I will send him over to cook a few good meals with the boys in the prison kitchen. You get three days of meals. If you're still not satisfied, we will talk again."

That same day, Dad assigned the family cook—a trusty—to the prison cafeteria. He knew Mom would be happy to cook our meals for a few days, especially because it meant the overall well-being of the prison counted on Dad's pre-emptive maneuver.

I remember that our cook made the best mashed potatoes and gravy. Luckily for me, there was a whole dinner's worth in the fridge before he left for the cafeteria. I hardly noticed his absence until I got a peanut butter sandwich in my lunch bag—usually it was roast beef.

Well, the three days of good food in the cafeteria must have satisfied the angry inmates, their bellies full of well-prepared food for the first time in months. The riot was called off and the cook came back to his normal hours at our house. The next day, I got a roast beef sandwich for lunch.

Chapter 16

Harry Orchard

Throughout my experience of being the warden's son, I met many inmates. Most of them made little impact on me, or on society, or even history. However, there was one inmate who had altered the course of Idaho history.

Harry Orchard was the most infamous criminal ever to be put in an Idaho prison. The locations of his crimes ranged from Michigan to Colorado to Idaho.

Occasionally, I would venture to the northern reaches of the prison grounds, close to the present location of the Idaho Botanical Gardens. There, I could find Orchard tending to the prison chickens and turkeys. He lived there by himself in a modest, yet comfortable, shack. By his own admittance, Orchard preferred isolation to being in the cells with other prisoners. His needs were simple, and he seemed very content with his self-imposed life of exile. Orchard had already been at the penitentiary for 37 years when my dad became warden. He was close to 80 years old when I first met him. White hair and looking a bit like a clean-shaven Santa Claus made him appear gentle. He may have been calm in his old age, but as a younger man, Orchard confessed to killing at least 17 people.

It may seem strange, but Orchard became quite close with my family and me. He was respected by Dad, and my mother would have conversations with him. On certain occasions, even my little sister was allowed to visit him, in the presence of a guard, of course. To add to his Santa Clause like demeanor, Orchard built a magnificent dollhouse for Pat and a wagon for me. He may not have been remorseful about the murders he committed, but he felt compassion toward children and those who meant him no harm.

Orchard seemed to have an insatiable curiosity, as only a person locked away from society might have. Whenever I would visit him, we would share information. I would tell him about the happenings of the outside world and he would permit limited questioning about his life in the early 1900s. From these encounters, I learned many things the rest of the world was not privy to about this notorious individual.

He was born in Ontario, Canada as Albert Horsely in March of 1866. Raised on a farm in poverty with seven brothers and sisters, he quit school after the third grade to work. In 1888, he left Ontario for the United States and started a business in Saginaw, Michigan. If I recall correctly, he was a cheesemaker with a wife and young daughter. Anyway, it proved to be a marginal business at best. Committing what may have been his first act of arson, Orchard burned down his factory and collected the insurance money. At the same time, he abandoned his family for another woman and ventured west. The affair lasted only a couple of months and Orchard did find some honest jobs, from driving a milk truck to working in the mines. But he couldn't resist gambling. Often deep in debt, he robbed a train depot, committed arson, sold fake life insurance policies, and rustled sheep. Along the way, he married and abandoned two more wives.

Eventually, he began a new career as a hired assassin in the violent Colorado Labor Wars of 1903-04. Working for the Western Federation of Miners, Orchard was paid to eliminate specific corporate structure supporters who opposed the miners' union.

On December 30, 1905, Orchard assassinated Idaho's former governor, Frank Stuenenberg, after placing a bomb at the fence of his home in Caldwell. Orchard was arrested two days later, eventually confessing to numerous crimes and murders.

From old records, I would learn more about Orchard's case and his trial which led to his life sentence. Clarence Darrow, a prominent lawyer of the time, was Orchard's defense attorney; William Borah and James H. Hawley on the prosecution team for what became known as Idaho's "Trial of the Century." Orchard pointed the finger at three union leaders who allegedly called for the assassination, including Big Bill Haywood. The trial lasted several years, the prosecution unable to convict the three orchestrators. However, in March 1908, Orchard was found guilty and sentenced to hang. Because he had cooperated with the prosecution, Orchard's sentence was altered to life in prison.

Apparently, Orchard became an institutionalized man rather quickly. He was converted to Seventh-day Adventism at the behest of Governor Stuenenberg's widow shortly after his conviction. From what I could tell, Orchard seemed content to stay in prison so long as someone kept him informed about the outside world. He enjoyed his post of watching the prison poultry.

When I was older, I researched the trial and had everything figured out. It was very complex, and it wasn't until years after personally knowing Orchard that I understood all the ins and outs of his case. But, when I was a child visiting the ramshackle hut he lived in, Orchard told me his side of the story. He had an interesting philosophy about it. According to Orchard, he felt like a soldier in a civil war between the union and the corporations. He explained that the purpose of his assassinations was to eventually bring about a successful end to the so-called civil war.

In our many conversations, I can't say he ever displayed any strong repentance or regret except for one horrible, unintentional murder. Even when I was young, Orchard told me the story in detail. His usual pre-bombing routine involved watching and following his target until he knew their daily schedules and routes. After observing an intended target for several weeks, Orchard placed a wire bomb in an empty lot to be triggered when the man walked through it on his way to work. Instead, Orchard watched in horror as a young girl on her way to school tripped the wire causing the bomb to explode. He was haunted by her death.

Orchard wrote two books while locked away. One restated his confessions and testimonies, the other explored his religious conversion. With no obvious desire or ability to reenter society, Orchard remained imprisoned until his death on April 13, 1954. His 46-year incarceration was the longest in Idaho history.

Harry Orchard poses during Idaho's "Trial of the Century" in 1907. (From left): Warden E. L. Whitney (Idaho State Penitentiary), Deputy Bartell (witness for state from Colorado), Orchard, Guard Ackley (Idaho State Pen), Ed Hawley (state), and Detective Charles Siringo (Pinkerton Agency). (Idaho State Archives)

Chapter 17

Pool or School

School was getting harder for me. Maybe because I was spending less
time on my studies and more time finding mischief.

When I was 13, my friends and I got into the habit of sneaking into a pool hall during our lunch hour. Sometimes we forgot to go back for afternoon classes. I don't know why we thought no one would notice, but we were learning more about shooting pool than anything being taught in school. I thought it was great fun until my dad found out.

"Jerry, do you have something to tell me?"

Apparently, Dad's idea of a proper way for his son to fill his days did not include hanging out in a pool hall. He decided that I needed a lesson in work ethic. In addition to school, I needed to get a job. One night, after I had finished my homework and helped clear the table, Dad and I sat down together with the *Idaho Statesman* classified section. There was an ad with a job opening for a bag boy at Albertsons, the local supermarket chain. At Dad's insistence, I applied. Even though I was only 13 and the minimum age for the job was 14, the store made an exception. Turns out my dad knew the manager.

From that point on, I worked after school every Monday, Tuesday and Wednesday. My shift was four hours each night. I also worked all day on Saturday's and Sunday's. This really cut into my pool-shooting time, but I would stay employed with Albertsons until I went to college. By the time I left, I was one of the youngest people at the Albertsons company to ever become a produce manager. See, I was a good kid.

Chapter 18

This Time I'm Leaving for Good

Many of the inmates felt they could laugh and joke with me. Some of them told me stories they wanted to share, but dared not tell guards, the Board of Corrections, or anyone else with authority. They confided in me and, for maybe the first five or six years of being close to them, I developed an empathy for them. I felt that they were downtrodden and suppressed. I believed that being confined to prison was a total inhumanity to man.

My father and I would sit at the dinner table and debate that issue. Of course, Dad's experience made him much more hardened and gradually I began to see his way of thinking. One of the things that changed my view, as I got older, was watching inmates come and go from the prison. When they were leaving, they would promise they would never again break the law and would never be back.

"I am never going through this again," they would promise.

Unfortunately, I would often wake up six months later to news that a former inmate was returning. I began to realize that they had a hard time accepting their own failures. They seemed to lay most of their problems on other people. In many of their minds, it was never their fault.

William Dreyer was an institutionalized man. He repeatedly told me that he was getting out for good and never coming back. However, he always came back. Bill's parole would be approved and shortly after being released he would be booked again. Like many repeat offenders, Dreyer thrived in the structured world of prison life but couldn't survive on the outside.

During Bill's stints as an inmate, he held several different job assignments. The first that I can recall was in the slaughterhouse located above the penitentiary in the foothills toward Table Rock. I would watch Bill bring cattle in from the ranches for slaughter, which he also performed.

I remember the day Bill was paroled and ready to leave the prison.

"It's been nice knowing you, Jerry," he said. "My path is going to be the straight and narrow."

As we waved to each other in the prison yard, I wondered if I would see him again. Next thing I knew, he was back.

This time, Dreyer was given a different prison occupation. He was not trained as a barber, but he was soon trimming everybody up. Guards, prisoners, even my dad and I would get our hair cut by Dreyer. The cost was 25 cents and it was just like going to any other barber.

Because Dreyer was a trusty, none of us hesitated to be near the man while he held a razor in his hand.

William Dreyer, 1935. (Idaho State Archives)

William Dreyer, 1937. (Idaho State Archives)

William Dreyer, 1938. (Idaho State Archives)

William Dreyer, 1942. (Idaho State Archives)

William Dreyer, 1945. (Idaho State Archives)

Chapter 19

Tarzan Takes Off

From the first night of my life at the prison, I knew escapes were a common occurrence. Many attempted and failed. Others didn't dare because they knew the consequences of being caught— longer sentences or solitary confinement for whatever length of time seemed appropriate. All but two were brought back to the prison during my dad's time as Warden.

Escapes were not limited to the male population of the prison. Women tried to escape all the time. The most memorable happened in the late evening hours of April 8, 1948. A young convicted murderer named Verna Keller (better known as Tarzan) and fellow inmate Margaret Barney climbed over the wall. Verna was only 17 years old and Margaret 21.

When the matron took roll call the next morning at six, they were noticeably missing from their cells. Upon further inspection, a note written by one of the two women flaunted their success in climbing over the walls. Apparently, the other female inmates doubted the two young women could pull it off. Going over the wall hadn't been done since Dad became warden; his guards were too good for that to happen. The note also said, "we'll be back soon." Not quite sure what to make of this, Dad stayed in his office while he sent several cars out to search the area.

Around eight that morning, Dad received a phone call.

"Hello, Verna Keller would like to make a collect call. Do you accept the charges?"

My dad accepted and waited for the young woman to get on the line.

"Good morning, Warden," Keller said casually. "I am sure you've noticed Margret and I aren't there right now."

"Yes, we have," Dad answered. "Verna, why are you calling?"

"Well, Warden, if you call off the police and stop searching for Margaret and me, we will be waiting for you to pick us up in Ontario."

Just across the Oregon border, Ontario was about 60 miles from Boise. Dad accepted the terms and they set a time to meet. Dad called off his search vehicles and got in his own car.

When he arrived in the pre-arranged place, the two women were waiting for him. They willingly got into the backseat and Dad drove back to the prison. Along the way, he asked them to explain their motivations and complimented them on their ingenuity—he thought their makeshift ladder was very clever.

"However," he told them. "You're going to be confined to your cells for this. No more freely walking around and building ladders or loosening bars on the windows."

Upon their return, the two women accepted their punishment. At least it wasn't the Hole or solitary confinement. They just couldn't go into the yard.

That night at dinner, Dad recounted the women's adventure to Mom, Pat and me. He animatedly told us about how they hitchhiked the two miles into Boise, late at night. From there, the women hitched another ride to Caldwell, where they stopped into a café and ate breakfast. After dining, the women convinced another man to drive them to Ontario where they got yet another ride back across the border to Payette, Idaho. Keller had called from Payette, which gave the two escapees enough time to return to Ontario before Dad arrived to get them. Dad was astounded by their ability to go so far in such a short amount of time. "They must have been traveling most of the night," he said.

At the end of his story, he looked at me. I must have had a puzzled look on my face because I was trying to recall something from the previous night. While I was sleeping, I thought I heard something outside my window. Assuming it was just a dream, I didn't look out the window to investigate. Suddenly, I realized it wasn't a dream.

"Dad," I said, my eyes wide with the realization. "I heard women giggling last night outside my window. I thought it was in a dream I was having. Do you think it was those inmates?"

Dad sighed and put his head in his hands, tired from another long day as warden.

Warden Clapp inspects the make-shift ladder used by Margaret Barney (top inset) and Verna Keller during their escape. (Idaho State Archives)

Chapter 20

Christmas Lights of 1950

One December night in 1950, I was out with my friends. We were old enough to drive; I was 16. We had been to a drive-in movie and for whatever reason, I was the first to be dropped off after the film ended. Maybe I had an earlier curfew than my friends. Like all teenage boys, my friends would tease one another. This night, they had been joking around more than usual and I knew I needed to get back at them for teasing me so mercilessly. As my friend drove up to the warden's residence, I plotted my revenge.

As we drove up the road, I sensed the fear of my three companions. The prison appeared ominous with the walls illuminated by floodlights, a stark contrast to the jolly looking trees near the house covered with Christmas lights. I did nothing to quiet their fears by cautioning them not to move too fast lest the tower guards shoot at them. I also liked to tease.

Now, the road at the prison was not wide enough to turn around. After letting me out, my friends had to drive north to a turn-around near the prison entry. I quickly dashed to the nearest decorated tree and unscrewed three or four big bulbs off a string of lights. Standing approximately 150 feet from the prison wall, hidden behind the tree, I waited for my friends to drive back down the road directly between me and the wall. As the car wheeled along at the sluggish pace that I had recommended, I readied my weapons. When my friend's car was even with the tree, I lobbed the bulbs, one after another, at the vehicle. Being the large, glass bulbs of that era, they made satisfying, but rather loud, popping sounds when they made impact with the car and road.

Against my somewhat false instructions, the driver immediately accelerated to a much higher speed, spraying snow and small rocks all over the road. I caught a glimpse of their faces as they flew by my hiding spot. Fear had gripped them; they were certain a tower guard had started shooting at the car. I thought myself to be rather clever and funny. I walked onto the porch, chuckling about my prank as I made my way to bed.

The next morning, being a Saturday, I was planning to sleep in until our houseboy came to my room at daybreak.

"Jerry, Warden wants to see you right away," he advised me.

Groggy and tired from being out late, I got up and started to get dressed.

"The warden said to hurry."

I combed my hair, brushed my teeth and slipped my leather loafers on without socks. My pajamas looked disheveled, but I was urged out of the house.

"Just get to the warden's office directly," the houseboy told me.

With a summons like that, I knew not to dilly-dally.

I walked to the administration building; my coat wrapped around me but definitely not covering the fact that I was still in my pajamas. I remember wondering what in the world would cause such urgency. There appeared to be much more activity with the guards and law enforcement persons coming and going. I looked at the bench outside my dad's office; it was full of inmates waiting for an audience with the warden. I asked the turnkey if I was truly required to be there. He confirmed that my dad has commanded that I be in his office. So, I took my spot on the bench beside an inmate to wait my turn. Several inmates came and went from the office. I sat on the bench for what seemed like an eternity. Another man arrived and sat beside me. Acutely aware of how ridiculous I looked in my winter coat, pajamas and loafers, I tried to ignore the man.

He looked me up and down before gruffly asking, "what're you in for?"

Luckily, I was called into the warden's office at that very moment. I hopped off the bench and found myself in the all-too familiar chair across from my dad who was sitting at his desk. Papers were piled neatly on each corner; the day's work was just beginning.

"Jerry, is there anything you want to tell me?"

I searched my memory for all the things I had done that week and could think of nothing to report. Before I could speak, my dad put a small box on the desk.

"Open it," he directed.

The box was very light and the contents made a soft tinkling sound. I lifted the lid to see pieces of broken Christmas lights.

"Jerry, is there something you want to tell me?"

I confessed.

"Do you realize, Jerry, that what you did last night caused me to have the entire prison searched?" Dad wasn't yelling at me, but his tone was stern and deep.

"We heard the explosions of those bulbs and thought gunshots were fired. My guards have been up all night, in a shakedown because of the racket you caused."

I apologized and took responsibility for my actions.

"Jerry, you're grounded," he commanded. "Thirty days. You may go back to the house and get dressed now."

I spent the next 30 days in my room, grounded from seeing my friends. At the time, I had not considered the possible consequences of my practical joke. I had crossed the boundary; not for the first time . . . or the last.

Pat sits on the steps of the Warden's House in December. (Courtesy of the Clapp Family)

Chapter 21

An Accidental Crime

Being a true Idaho boy, one of my favorite hobbies was hunting. Influenced by Dad, Chris the houseboy, Davy Crockett, and all the famous cowboys, and their Indian chief counterparts, I often embarked on hunting and fishing adventures. Occasionally, like our trip to the dude ranch when I was 11 years old, we hunted and fished as a family. As I got a little bit older—and more capable of handling a shotgun—I would venture off to hunt alone. I liked it better that way sometimes. It was quiet and peaceful. There wasn't much big game hunting in Boise, but the bird hunting was usually pretty good, especially on Eagle Island. In fact, because my dad oversaw the prison farm out there, he had arranged for them to set up various duck blinds along the river on either side of the island. This gave me twice as much room for duck and goose hunting on weekends.

One sunny day, feeling called by the wild, I decided to leave school after lunch and spend my time elsewhere. I knew my dad would hear about my absence from school, but at least he couldn't fault me for going to the pool hall. At the farm, Bull Gang guards would keep an eye on me and make sure I stayed out of trouble. My thought was that I might not get into trouble if I brought home a goose to cook for dinner. I hopped in my car and started driving west toward the prison farm.

It was late fall. The leaves had created a dense carpet on the ground all over the island. The prison workers were cleaning up the vast gardens, preparing them for next spring. The Boise River, which flows on both sides of the island, was low and flowing with a delicate current, the reflection of the sky and overhanging trees crisp and clear on the water's surface. I threw on my thick wool hunting jacket, grabbed my shotgun, and made my way to the shoreline. As I walked, Bull Gang members waved at me and a few of the guards greeted me.

"Hey Jerry, bringing home dinner tonight?"

I joked with them for a moment and told a few of the guards where I planned to locate myself, so they didn't think I was a prisoner trying to escape. Finally, I reached my favorite duck blind and began settling in.

I breathed in the cool autumn air. It was a quiet day on the farm; the surrounding area had not yet been developed into neighborhoods, so the silence was pervasive as I waited for a target to come my way. There were small birds chirping and flitting around, squirrels were dashing about gathering whatever seeds and nuts were left to be found. They were all preparing for the first major freeze and the winter that would quickly follow. I watched the activity with mild interest because my sight was mostly cast on the river and the waterfowl that would hopefully be making an appearance soon.

Not entirely sure how much time had gone by, I finally saw a large, white bird flying low over the water. I had heard the gentle flap and splash of water as the bird dipped the tips of its wings into the river. I readied my shotgun. I took a deep breath. Took aim. I exhaled at the same time I pulled the trigger. BANG! The shotgun fired loudly, breaking the silence that had encased the island. All the smaller birds shrieked and dispersed in a rush. The squirrels scattered, hiding in their nests. My aim had been good. A second after pulling the trigger, I heard a loud splash as the bird hit the water. I could see it bobbing, the buoyancy of its feathers and body fat preventing it from sinking. Not wanting the dead waterfowl to be completely waterlogged, I waded out into the low river to retrieve it rather than waiting for the current to bring it close to me.

Upon reaching it, I admired its soft white feathers. I had just shot a snow goose! These were rare this time of year and from what I had heard they were very delicious. Excited about my achievement, I prepared to take it home. Getting it to shore was easy, the water supported most of the surprisingly large fowl's weight for me. Once I pulled it to land, however, it was quite heavy. *That's okay,* I thought, *just more meat to enjoy.* Paying no attention to the distinct lack of any gray or black feathers on the wings—a telling trait of snow geese—I began dragging the dead bird to my car which was parked on the other side of the island.

I wouldn't say I struggled to pull the dead weight of that bird from one side of the island to the other, but I wouldn't say it was easy either. When I reached my vehicle and prepared to load the snow goose into the trunk, I noticed the neck had gotten quite a bit longer than it was when I first shot it. I assumed this was due to me pulling the body by its head and the muscles and bones in the neck had simply loosened or dislocated along the way. Heaving the body into my trunk, I was still very pleased with my hunting trophy. I congratulated myself all the way home for bringing in such a rare species this time of year.

Upon arriving back at the penitentiary, I drove straight to the administration building after turning left off Warm Springs Road. I could not contain my enthusiasm any longer—I had to show dad what I shot. I was going to conveniently leave out the part about skipping school with the hope that he would be so proud of my hunting abilities, he wouldn't notice or at least not mention the timing of the event. After parking my car and going inside the administration building, I turned right into my dad's office. He and Chief Deputy Warden O'Neil were there talking. They both looked up and smiled when I knocked on the door frame. After exchanging a quick greeting with both, I told them I had been hunting and got the most amazing trophy at the prison farm.

"If you aren't too busy, come look!"

Dad and O'Neil followed me out to the car, interested in what could possibly be so thrilling. As I escorted them, I told them the story of the large, graceful, white bird flying down the river. Before I popped the trunk of my car, I proudly announced, "I shot a snow goose!"

Dad was excited to see my prized bird. The trunk opened. The bird was fully visible for just seconds before O'Neil slammed the trunk shut again. Confused, I looked at O'Neil who was leaning with both hands on the trunk of my car.

Through the tobacco in his cheek he whispered, "Jesus Christ, Warden. Jerry shot a trumpeter swan."

Dad's face went slightly pale.

"No, that's a snow goose," I protested.

Dad asked O'Neil to stand aside so he could get a better look at the dead bird inside my vehicle. Opening the trunk just enough to see inside, my dad peered in and nodded.

"You're right, Pat," Dad whispered. "That's a swan. How could you not tell the difference, Jerry? There are no black feathers on its wings." I was slightly dumbfounded and speechless. I knew this was not a good turn of events, but O'Neil vocalized just how bad it was.

"This is an illegal kill," he said. "The fine for killing a swan is $10,000."

My heart sank into my stomach and I began to worry about how many hours I would have to work at Albertsons to cover the cost of the fine.

"Don't panic, son," Dad said quietly, ushering me toward the driver's seat of my car. "Just take it home, get it inside without anyone noticing and we'll take care of it. We'll cook it up for dinner and no one will be the wiser."

Following my dad's orders, I got it home. Now that my joy had been destroyed, I took the bird straight to the cook. The next day, after the "snow goose" had been feathered and cleaned and roasted in the oven for a good chunk of the afternoon, our cook served it for dinner. Not wanting this poor swan's life to be wasted, I suffered through eating it. The meat was tough and chewy. No amount of gravy could hide the texture . . . or cover the taste of lingering guilt I felt for mistaking a swan for a goose.

Lou Clapp inspects the infamous car trunk. (Courtesy of the Clapp Family)

Chapter 22

A Foundation for Reading

During my high school years, my time to socialize was limited. At night, after my Albertsons' shift was complete and my homework done, I often found myself getting lost in books. Because I had always enjoyed reading, it became a staple to my personal entertainment.

My taste in books diverted from my friends' choices. I was a little more intense. I loved everything by Lloyd C. Douglas, delving into *The Robe* and *The Big Fisherman*. His storytelling captured my imagination. I also read a lot of material about prisons. I would find collections of documents; anything connected with prisons. I particularly liked things written by prisoners. I often used what I learned from these books in my high school speech classes. Any time I could relate my passion for prison books to my schoolwork, I would. Luckily, my teachers would often assign presentations or papers about prisons and crimes or war.

Chapter 23

A Very Thirsty Inmate

On quiet nights, we could occasionally hear screams and shouts from both sides of the prison. The men were not often loud because they knew there were bad repercussions if they made noise after lights out. The women, on the other hand, were not punished so severely. If they caused enough commotion, they would be released to the state mental hospital in Blackfoot. Not that the mental hospital was a lot better than prison, but some women might have felt that this alternative was preferable. The main reason anyone from the prison tried to be admitted to Blackfoot was because of the possibility they could be deemed sane and released back into society.

However, that wasn't easy. Getting into the mental hospital required being screened by the doctors there. If there didn't seem to be anything wrong with an inmate, they were sent back to the prison. Sometimes, they would be transferred back and forth multiple times before a final decision was made.

Situations like that did not happen often because of the required punishments, but on one such occasion, a woman screamed for several days. She screamed for water constantly. The woman wanted to be transferred to Blackfoot, but the warden refused. My dad and the matron had done everything they could to quiet the woman from screaming, but nothing seemed to placate her. They locked her up in an attempt to keep the other inmates of the women's ward from harming her. Her screams were annoying everyone within earshot.

We could hear her screaming from the house, day in and day out.

"I've had it with that woman!" Dad finally exclaimed, slamming both of his fists on the table one night during dinner. "She is driving me crazy. I'm the one who's going to end up in Blackfoot if she keeps on."

My mother probably told him he was over-reacting. The screaming was annoying, but we could live with it. The inmate would eventually wear herself out.

"I've had her sent to Blackfoot, they have evaluated her," Dad said. "There is nothing wrong with her and they keep sending her back!"

Aggravated, my dad put his head in his hands for a moment and rubbed his eyes.

"I guess I better do something. Come on, Jerry, let's go. Thank you for dinner."

We stood up from the table; I wasn't sure what to expect from this impromptu trip to the women's ward. As he usually did before entering the women's facility, Dad gathered two trusties. The four of us went to the supply shed and procured a fire hose. Dad hooked one end of the hose to the hydrant closest to the women's ward and unrolled the hose all the way to the screaming woman's cell. Placing it on the floor, Dad spoke to the female inmates.

"If she screams or asks for water one more time," he said sternly. "Turn on the hose and give her all the water she wants."

He turned and stared directly into the screaming woman's face. She had gone silent when my dad walked in with the hose. She trembled under his gaze, not uttering a sound. Dad turned and left the building, putting his arm around my shoulder to guide me out.

The woman never again asked for a transfer to the mental hospital. Until the day she left the prison, she was quiet and well-mannered.

Chapter 24

The Barber is Back

You remember Bill Dreyer, the prison barber with a penchant for being released and then returning.

At one point in my teen years, Dreyer had been gone for several months and my hair was looking a right mess. So, when I went to see the prison barber, I really expected he would be a new trusty.

"Bill, it is nice to see you again," I said, genuinely surprised. "I've got to have a haircut."

"It's always good to see you, too, Jerry," Dreyer chuckled as he draped the smock over my shoulders while I settled into the barber chair.

Luckily, Dreyer had a good sense of humor and he liked youngsters. He would always tell stories and joke around with me while he trimmed my hair.

"So, can you tell me what happened this time?" I asked him, knowing I was about to have my ear talked off. "You must have been out for three or four months this time. Where were you?"

"I decided I needed a change of scenery," Dreyer stated matter-of-factly. "I went to Texas. I spent a couple of months down there. But I got concerned about what would happen if I fell in Texas. I knew I didn't want to fall in Texas, even though I nearly did."

He explained that "to fall" was an inmate term, or slang, for violating parole. And according to Dreyer, falling in Texas was never a pleasant experience because they run such tough institutions.

"Tell me about what happened," I said, urging him to get on with the story.

"Okay, okay," he said. "I was out one night robbing a place. I had stuffed all the valuables I could find into a pillowcase and tossed it over my shoulder, but as I was leaving, the police stopped me in the alleyway. I was totally caught red-handed. They marched me downtown to the jail and booked me."

I could tell he was setting the stage for a great story because his barber scissors were snipping dangerously close to my ear.

"There were maybe four or five other men in the cell with me," he continued. "I looked around and noticed a very drunk man passed out on the bench. I sat down next to him and, when nobody was looking, started rifling through his pockets. Wouldn't you just know it, I found his driver's license. Knowing I had just hit the jackpot, I waited patiently until morning when the turnkey arrived and called the drunk man's name for release. Well, the drunk guy was still passed out, so I walked up to the window and presented his driver's license. Without any questions, the turnkey let me go and I left the drunk man on his bench."

Stunned by the wild story, I sat in the chair thinking about that poor drunk man.

"So, Bill, do you have any idea what happened to the guy whose license you stole?"

"I always felt regretful for potentially causing a bad situation for him; and sometimes wondered what went down," Dreyer said. "But I did not stay in town long enough to find out."

Chapter 25

The Double Hanging of 1951

Growing up in the situation that I did gave me a very strong opinion about capital punishment. My father instilled in me his own beliefs, as many parents do. He told me that the last form of rehabilitation was execution.

As warden, Dad worked hard to rehabilitate as many inmates as he could. Rehabilitation requires a change in behavior and way of life; sometimes it is possible for a criminal to turn his or her life around and be a productive member of society. However, when rehabilitation does not seem to be an option, the choices are either life in prison or the death penalty.

The gravity of an execution weighed heavily on my dad throughout his term as warden. Part of his responsibility at the prison was his position as chairman of the three-person Board of Corrections. In 1951, when two executions were proposed, one member of the board voted against hangings because of his religion and the other voted in favor, leaving the warden as the ultimate tiebreaker. The decision took Dad several days to make. He would pace through the house at all hours of the night. I could hear his footsteps and the creak of floorboards as he wrestled with his innermost thoughts. During his deliberation, Dad told me about his conflictions.

"This is the toughest part of my job as warden so far," he said. "If I do vote for an execution, I have to be present. I have to administer the whole thing."

Dad was open to me about what it meant to administer capital punishment. Ultimately, he rationalized the act of execution.

"The problem," Dad cogitated during one of our conversations, "is that some people, if allowed to live, will kill again. Perhaps another inmate or a guard, or me. Or you or your sister. The only way to secure a future where that can't happen is for an inmate to be sent to the gallows."

In Idaho, hanging was the method of executing the death penalty. Lethal injection would not be implemented until the late 1970s, almost a decade after my dad left his position at the prison.

In 1944, prior to my dad's appointment, the ominous and excruciating gallows were built in the center of the prison yard. The presence of even temporary gallows instilled so much anxiety in the prison population, Dad felt it inhumane for them to be built where everyone could watch. He also believed that being put to death was horrible enough without hundreds of eyes watching. Likewise, he felt it unfair to force the inmates who had not committed such atrocities as cold-blooded murder to watch as their fellows plummeted to their deaths.

Even though I have already described a variety of grim details about growing up around a prison, it would be on a chilling Friday the 13th that I would see something truly gruesome. Imagine being a young adult—just turned 17 years old—and witnessing the aftermath of capital punishment. I will do my best not to be too graphic, but the image of what I saw on that stormy, eerie Friday night—April 13, 1951—has haunted me my entire life.

I had become accustomed to walking past Death Row on my way to the prison barbershop. The small, unforgiving cells had been vacant for a while. Without occupants, the cells were innocuous, just empty space.

One day, while I was walking to my haircut, the guard outside Cell Block No. 1 stopped me before I entered.

"Jerry," the guard said, looking me square in the eyes to reflect importance. "We booked Walrath and Powell into Death Row since your last visit to the barber."

Of course, I knew this. I had witnessed Dad pacing for several days before making the difficult decision. I nodded that I understood.

"They are pretty calm," the guard continued, "unless you stare at them. So, when you go inside, just keep your eyes on the ground in front of you. Any eye contact might set them off."

Feeling a little more jittery than I had felt within the prison walls in a long time, I proceeded to the barbershop. As I entered Cell Block 1, the Death Row cells were located directly in front of the door, making it difficult to not look straight into the inhabitant's faces.

I passed through the doorway, not really sure what to expect from the two young men locked behind some of the thickest bars in the penitentiary. Unlike solitary confinement, the prisoners on Death Row could see and be seen, but their time outside of the cells was incredibly restricted—an hour a day tops when no one else was in the yard—and heavily guarded. Because these men were new to Death Row, I thought they might yell, scream or bang on the bars while I walked by. The guard at the entrance had made me nervous; picturing the two as incredibly dangerous and insane. As I got closer to the turn that would lead me to the barber, I took the quickest, sneakiest of peeks at Ernest Walrath, contained in the first cell, and Troy Powell, in the second. They were hardly older than I was—maybe four or five years my senior. The young men sat in silence, sadly watching as I freely walked past their cells. They made no noise.

After my haircut, I finished my conversation with Bill Dreyer and handed him his 25-cent token. I heard some guards entering the building; they were talking loudly and jeering at the men on Death Row. Intentionally intimidating the men, the guards referenced the imminent executions.

"They're going to hang you, you know," one of them said.

"Yeah, watch the murderers swing from the rope," the other interjected.

I hurried past the guards and the cells. Obviously, I knew being on Death Row meant you had done something truly horrific and there was no hope of rehabilitation, but to be subject to inescapable ridicule in the last days of your life seemed like adding salt to the wound. It didn't sit well with me.

On my way back to the house, I stopped by Dad's office. I wanted to ask him why the guards tormented Walrath and Powell so badly.

"You know their crime, Jerry," Dad said. "People are angry and feel those boys deserve what's coming to them."

Dad had shown me pictures of the victim's body prior to this conversation. Walrath and Powell had been convicted of murdering a well-known grocer named Newton Wilson in East Boise while robbing his home. Walrath went into the situation brandishing a defective gun at Wilson. When he tried to fire it, the weapon malfunctioned and didn't shoot. Powell, who didn't want to rely on a firearm, had brought a sap—sock filled with rocks— along with him.

When the gun didn't fire, Powell had bashed Wilson on the head with the sap, rendering the grocer unconscious. As Wilson lay there, Powell ready to beat him again if he moved, Walrath searched the kitchen for a butcher knife. Walrath then stabbed Wilson to death. It was determined the killing was premeditated, thus the conviction of murder in the first degree and the sentence of death by hanging. During the robbery, Walrath and Powell obtained just $12.50 from Wilson's home.

The day of Walrath and Powell's double execution quickly approached. Their attorney, Jess Hawley, fought hard for them, firmly believing that Powell should be spared the gallows for life in prison. Hawley argued that Powell had been influenced by Walrath into assisting in the robbery. Plus, it had been Walrath who carried out the murder. Hawley lost the case. Walrath and Powell were set to be hanged at midnight on Friday the 13th.

The gallows were constructed, attendants were selected, and an executioner was brought in from Oregon. As I recall, the professional hangman had executed more than 30 individuals during his career. Lovell Painter—a guard—volunteered to be the trap-man. These names were kept very confidential and I only learned about them because my dad had recently begun to include me in his confidentiality.

Dad explained the execution process to me. After a final meal which Powell and Walrath agreed could be whatever the other prisoners were having; my dad, the inmate, and the hangman would stand on the scaffold. My dad would ask the inmate if he had anything to say and the inmate could say whatever he wanted or nothing at all.

"Lord, Jesus, receive my spirit," Walrath said.

The hangman then placed the noose over the neck and snapped the knot to the left side of Walrath's head just behind his ear, rendering him unconscious. At the same time, the hangman nodded to the trap-man to release the door beneath the inmate's feet. Walrath's unconscious body fell through the trap where two doctors waited below to confirm the death.

Dr. Wahle, the prison physician, had climbed up a step stool to reach the dangling body. When the doctor held his stethoscope on Walrath's chest, the dead man's legs and arms suddenly raised up, nearly knocking the doctor off the ladder. Apparently, the cold stethoscope when placed upon the man's chest had caused rigor mortis to quickly set in. Walrath was pronounced dead at 12:22 a.m., but Dr. Wahle was so shaken by the incident that Clyde Summers, the Ada County Coroner, had to give him a tranquilizer. After moving the prison doctor away from the gallows to settle him down, Summers now took the responsibility to check the second body coming through the trap door.

"I know I'm right with God," would be the 21-year-old Powell's last words.

The door was triggered for a second time and Coroners Summers and McMurtrey declared Powell dead at 12:50am. Powell was 21 years old, Walrath 22.

I remember that night vividly. A storm had rolled in, the clouds covered the quarter moon and blocked out any light. Trees shook as wind blew through their branches. But despite the blustery weather, the prison was completely silent. Dad had offered to let me watch the hangings, but I chose to decline. The grim situation weighed heavily on us all.

Feeling uneasy just sitting in the living room with my mother and sister, I had left the house and entered the prison moments before the executions. Sitting quietly with a few guards outside the prison wall in a tunnel by the warden's office, I saw Coroner McMurtrey bring the covered gurney holding Walrath's body out through the turnkey's office. As the coroner waited for the gate to open, I was standing right beside the body when a guard walked up.

"I didn't see the execution," said the guard, who then, without any warning, pulled back the sheet.

I will never forget what I saw. Where the rope had tightened, Walrath's neck was one inch in diameter. It was grotesque. I rushed to the bathroom. I was so sick. I vowed to never be near another hanging again.

Ernest Walrath. (Idaho State Archives)

Troy Powell. (Idaho State Archives)

100

Chapter 26

A Troubled Guard

Lovell A. Painter had seen a lot in his short life. An Army private during World War II, he was wounded in Germany and was undoubtedly wrought with post-traumatic stress disorder, though that was never confirmed. In early 1944, when Painter returned to Idaho from the war, his family assisted him in finding a new pathway. Shortly before being hired by my dad to be a prison guard, Painter tried his hand as a sheepherder in Grand View. I don't recall if that was the family trade or if he wanted to have a quiet existence after being subjected to the horrors taking place across the Atlantic. Regardless, herding sheep did not suit him.

On a drive between Boise and Mountain Home, my dad told me a story and showed the hill on which Painter caused quite a scandal. While Painter was herding his sheep with another man, the two shepherds began to argue. Becoming physical, Painter pushed the other man down on a hill and demanded that he crawl back to town. To enforce this, Painter drew a gun and fired it between the other man's hands and knees as he crawled back to Grand View.

Despite feeling skeptical that my dad's story was accurate, I knew Painter was quick and deadly accurate with a gun. One day, an unsuspecting deer ran by the prison wall and, without hesitation, Painter killed it with one shot from the tower.

Painter was polite, but quiet and a little strange. Everyone chalked it up to his time in Europe during combat and always being on edge since coming home. As a guard, Painter didn't care if anyone liked him so long as he was respected. He wasn't shy about being tough.

Every prisoner understood they should never attempt escape while Painter was on duty. I also kept my distance from him.

As I mentioned, he volunteered as the trap man during the double hanging in 1951. The following spring, Painter's life took an odd turn. My memory of how it happened is not very clear—I had my mind on other things, like my job as a bag boy and the cute girls in my class at school. I just recall things started going very badly for Painter and were swiftly getting worse.

In early January of 1952, Painter went to a bar in downtown Boise to do some drinking. I do remember that his choice of beverage was Rainier, a popular beer brewed in Seattle. Considering that Boise was still a small city, it was not unusual for guards and previously incarcerated men to occasionally stumble upon each other at the common watering holes. Most guards, however, would do no more than nod to a man they recognized and move on. Painter followed this procedure when he was out on the town, speaking to old inmates only if need be. But one evening proved very different.

An ex-inmate by the name of Delmar Theodore Swatsenbarg saw Painter at the bar and got a nasty itch to stir up trouble. Being a "two-time loser" at the prison, the 36-year-old Swatsenbarg had seen his fair share of Painter's guarding methods and seemed to think this would be a good time to display retaliation for the treatment he had received while behind bars. I'm not implying that Painter was a violent or dangerous guard; my dad would never allow that. But, again, he was simply tougher than most and would put inmates in their place if they got out of line under his watch.

Painter, upon feeling uncomfortable following the brief encounter with Swatsenbarg, decided to quietly leave the crowded pub. Feeling tipsy and slightly disoriented from drinking and the noise of the bar, he hailed a taxi. One pulled over and Painter told the driver a destination. Opening the door to the back seat, Painter was shoved from the side and roughly pushed into the vehicle by Swatsenbarg, who held a gun to Painter and barked instructions to the cab driver.

"Drive out to Rocky Bar," Swatsenbarg demanded. "I've got a gun, so no funny business or I'll blow both your guts out right here."

Painter knew better than to test this man and bided his time while they took the bumpy, abandoned road. When the taxi reached Rocky Bar, the driver pulled the car to a stop. Snow was falling in front of the headlights glowing brightly in the darkness. Swatsenbarg poked Painter in the ribs with the gun.

"Get out," he grumbled.

Painter pushed the back door open. It swung wide due to the vehicle being parked on a steep hill. Looking around, Painter saw a rock on the ground and pretended to stumble out of the car to reach for it. As Swatsenbarg shuffled out of the car, he momentarily looked at the ground to get his footing on the hill. At that moment, Painter raised his arm up and brought the rock crashing down on his captor's head.

Dazed, Swatsenbarg began to grapple with Painter, ultimately causing both men to collapse into the snow and tumble down the slope. They rolled, hitting sagebrush buried by snow, feeling large rocks under their backs as they descended, still punching. When the cab driver reached the bottom of the hill, Painter was still pounding the unconscious ex-con. Eventually, the driver was able to pull Painter from the almost lifeless body. Both of the fighters were caked in each other's blood.

"He's still breathin," the cab driver said. "Christ, I've never seen another fight like that. What should we do?"

"Grab his feet," ordered Painter. "We'll drive him to the hospital." After an arduous trek back up the hill carrying Swatsenbarg's limp and unconscious body, Painter and the driver laid him across the back seat. Painter took control of the weapon and held it on the former prisoner in case he regained consciousness on the way to the Boise hospital.

Eventually, Swatsenbarg recovered, was indicted for kidnapping and attempted murder, and was sent back to the state penitentiary. The scar on Swatsenbarg's head from Painter's rock never fully faded.

Painter had deeper wounds. Several months after the attempted murder, he was still understandably shaken. Dad mentioned that Painter made recurring visits to his office, complaining of feeling jumpy and nervous.

On Thursday night—May 29, 1952—Painter went to his favorite bar, drank heavily and brandished his weapon. This was plainly against regulations and Painter was escorted out of the establishment by local police, who reminded him of his responsibility.

"Never carry a gun while away from prison property," one of the officers said. "You know it's too dangerous."

After being notified by the police of Painter's transgressions, my dad got a call from the guard, who sounded intoxicated and highly agitated.

"I need to quit working at the penitentiary," Painter said.

"I accept your resignation," Dad told him. "But you need to come directly to my office to turn in your weapons and uniforms."

"Yeah, okay Warden," Painter mumbled on the other end of the line. "Be there soon."

However, rather than making his way back to the prison, Painter pocketed his prison sanctioned weapon and started walking further into downtown Boise. Around 5 p.m., another prison guard encountered Painter pacing up and down Main Street. After politely greeting the noticeably upset Painter, the guard was looking into the barrel of Painter's gun. The guard could not remember exactly what Painter said to him, but he knew it was a death threat. Quick to think about his training at the prison, the guard started to talk Painter down.

"I promise I'll do whatever you want me to do," the man told Painter. "Just please let me go without injury."

Painter agreed to let him go, but then continued his bizarre mission in the heart of Boise while the released guard rushed to contact authorities about the strange and frightening confrontation.

Still on Main Street, moving two blocks west, Painter entered a service station and immediately held his gun on the attendant.

"Call the Boise FBI office," Painter demanded. "When you get them on the line, verify that I am an FBI agent."

As the frightened attendant followed instructions, asking the phone operator to connect him with the FBI, Painter never once looked away or lowered the weapon. Shaking slightly and sweating profusely, Painter muttered under his breath for the attendant to hurry up with the call.

When the FBI answered, Painter's hostage explained the situation as calmly as he could and provided an address. Hearing police sirens in the distance, Painter booked it out of the service station and tried to run down Main Street. A police car swerved in front of him, blocking his way. Without anywhere to go, Painter was apprehended by the police and taken to the station.

I was shocked when Dad told us at dinner that night. Naturally, the newspapers were all over the story. "Prison Guard Faces Charge of Assault with Deadly Weapon" was one of the headlines.

Boise police officers who later spoke to the media said that Painter was "'irrational'" following his arrest. Jailers and those who questioned him corroborated the story. Like the detectives who investigated the case, no one could make any sense of the situation. The whole time I had known him, Painter seemed like an average man, a little quiet and standoffish but average.

Ultimately, Painter was sent to the state hospital in Blackfoot. One of the doctors said that Painter "had been delirious since he was brought to hospital, but there appeared to be nothing physically wrong."

On June 7, 1952, newspapers briefly and unceremoniously reported that "Lovell A. Painter, former Idaho state prison guard, died of a bleeding ulcer." Painter was only 45 years old.

Guard tower at the Idaho State Penitentiary. (Idaho State Archives)

Chapter 27

The Spring Riot of 1952

I remember Red, the houseboy, running to our house without warning.

"Warden, warden," he was shouting from a distance.

Dad and I met him on the porch.

"Warden, you gotta come quick," Red huffed, trying to catch his breath. "It's hell in there . . . a major riot is starting!"

Shuffling me back into the house, Dad reached for the hallway telephone, contacting local law enforcement to get to the prison immediately.

"It's a riot this time," he said. "Bring everything you can spare." Dad paused for a moment while the other person on the line spoke. "Yes, please spread the word. I think we will need everyone we can get. Thank you."

Dad then rushed over to his office and the entrance to the prison. I could hear raucous yelling from within the walls. Every few minutes there were loud crashes; the distinct sound of glass shattering as heavy objects were thrown through it. How we had missed all this noise before Red notified us is beyond me. I left the doorway and stood on the porch, listening to the madness taking control inside the walls of the penitentiary. Sirens in the distance got louder and louder as law enforcement arrived to help quell the situation. I watched as each police and sheriff car flew down the road, screeching to a stop outside the gates of the prison. My dad calmly, but swiftly, briefed all the officers. I was too far away to hear what he told them.

The word had certainly spread. As the day wore on, officers arrived from as far away as Jerome to the south and Weiser to the west. This was the first riot in over a decade: it was not to be missed by anyone. From the porch, I could see civilians perched on the top of Table Rock, watching the riot unfold inside the sandstone walls. Those thrill-seekers wanted to be close to the action, but far enough away to be out of danger should anything go further awry.

I deserted the porch, creeping closer to the prison walls. I couldn't see what was happening, but the noise was deafening. I walked along the wall leading to the heating plant, my hand stretched out to touch the sandstone bricks, all the while I kept looking up in order to spot the tower guards. I found it unusual that they were not in their towers—they were always in the towers. When I got to the junction of the west and south walls, I looked up at the catwalk along the south wall and saw Dad, surrounded by heavily armed law officers, with a megaphone.

"If you don't come out in ten minutes," he commanded, "we will open fire."

From my position, I could now see a portion of the prison yard. It looked as though approximately 250 inmates—almost half of the prison population—had seized control of the single-story recreation hall. They had destroyed the prison laundry, shoe shop, the license plate manufacturing facility and the "loafer hall". Several of the rioting convicts also set fire to an unfinished cellblock only to be thwarted by its previously installed sprinkler system. To add to the pandemonium inside the wall, more than half of the inmates were armed with hatchets, knives, wrecking bars and billy-clubs they had clearly stolen from guards.

One guard later recalled doing a routine check and being met at a cellblock entrance by a group of inmates who took his keys and club, threatening to hold him hostage during the riot. After narrowly escaping that fate, the guard had notified others of the imminent uprising of prisoners.

Stationing myself with the best vantage point possible, I looked to my left and right. I had not been the only spectator to find an observation point along this wall. Reporters started gathering soon after law enforcement arrived. Over the noise from within, I could hear reporters who had managed to find a safe place along the wall asking non-participating prisoners for their opinion about what was happening. I heard some inmates say that they were dissatisfied with the grievance committee and that they didn't get enough recreation. I could also make out complaints about guards who "kicked guys, beat 'em and called them dirty names."

Being terrified and completely engaged in the scene before me, time had stood still. Obviously more aware of the moments ticking by, my dad attempted to negotiate with the inmates again. He had already given them ten minutes to surrender.

"You've wasted ten minutes already," Dad spoke matter-of-factly over the megaphone. "You can either waste another ten minutes or surrender now."

Ten more minutes were placed on the table for rioters. Rather than surrendering, three members of the prison population came out of the destroyed building with their own negotiation tactics. They were members of a four-person grievance committee within the prison; the facilitators of this uprising.

"We won't come out without a fair hearing for those boys you've got in lockup," one of the leaders said, also demanding that none of the inmates be held responsible for the riot. The negotiator also requested to conduct a hearing in the presence of newsmen. My dad continued to listen while the men listed their demands.

"Well, boys, I'm afraid none of those things are going to happen," Dad said, refusing to release the "ringleaders" from solitary confinement or meet any of the inmates' demands.

Everything turned from very, very bad to absolute chaos at this news. After waiting for another tense fifteen minutes, my dad looked at his watch. It was 2:55 p.m.

"You were warned," he shouted into his megaphone.

Placing a pair of heavy-duty, military-grade earmuffs over his head, Dad turned to the men who had their guns trained inside the wall.

"Fire," he ordered as the men braced themselves.

A series of extraordinarily BOOMS permeated the air. Immediately covering my ears, I noticed the reporters had dropped their notebooks and pens while trying to protect their ears. The men holding the weapons and other law enforcement officers sported protective earmuffs; the rest of us were forced to hope there would be no lasting damage to our hearing. Instinctively, I had dropped closer to the ground when the firing began. Crouched on the balls of my feet, knees at my chin, hands covering my ears, I was not well balanced. But fear, powerful curiosity and exhilaration kept me from bolting for home. From where I was, I could see large projectiles coming from the guns and hear screams coming from the yard. A faint smell wafted over the wall, stinging my eyes and throat. The reporters close to me were coughing, also affected by the stinging fumes.

For about ten minutes, the armed men fired tear gas bombs into the prison yard. They aimed for the multipurpose building where the prisoners were taking shelter. The yells and booms were accompanied by the sound of bricks crashing to the ground. More windows were shattered, the glass tinkling as it made impact with the ground. The building, all but decimated, no longer offered shelter for the inmates. During the continuous blasts, every one of the rioters ran onto the softball field. Coughing and wheezing, their eyes watering horribly, the 250 prisoners were forced to surrender.

"Lay down on the ground and don't move," Dad's voice blared

from the megaphone.

Satisfied no one inside was about to move another muscle, my dad had the armed men lower their weapons. The riot was over.

When everything was safe and settled in the yard and the inmates had been returned to their cells, the press began asking my dad questions and prying information out of other officers. It seemed like everyone was taking pictures of my dad. The fearless Warden Louis E. Clapp had ended a five-hour riot with no casualties. I had to push my way through the crowd of reporters. Once I got to Dad's side, he clapped me on the shoulder.

"Let's go look at the damage," he said, leading myself and all the newspaper reporters inside the wall.

First, we went into the license plate factory which had been destroyed by the rioters. Debris was scattered everywhere. It was so bad that the manufacture of Idaho's new 1953 license plates would be set back nearly two months.

Next, we went into the commissary where all the cigarettes, candy and pop had been ransacked and taken by the inmates. In the rush to rob the commissary, some items had been left behind and trampled. Cigarettes had been dropped and smashed, wrappers and tobacco scattered on the counter tops. Candy bars also lay in the dirt, caked in dust, slightly protruding from their wrappers after being stepped on in the prisoners' haste.

Lastly, my dad led everyone into the loafing area where we could all smell the lingering tear gas. As if the damage done by prisoners hadn't been extensive enough, the tear gas bombs had caused their own destruction. Those bombshells were strong; most of them had penetrated the wire screens in the area and eight of the spent gas shells went through the entire building. They were found lying on the ground on the far side of the recreation hall, opposite of where the gas squad fired them. Overall, a total of 64 gas shells had been fired into the recreation hall where the rioting convicts had barricaded themselves. For the shells, the state police would charge the penitentiary $625.16.

Many of the inmates were now in the prison hospital because of the tear gas they had inhaled during the riot, their eyes burning and watering. Those who were exposed to excessive amounts were having difficulty breathing and some complained of chest pains. The convicts closest also suffered some skin irritation, almost like mild burns. My dad and state police superintendent A. P. Bunderson both agreed that it was amazing that none of the bombs or shells had hit any inmates.

"We were pretty lucky in not hurting somebody at that," the state police superintendent said on record. "When you consider that there were 250 to 300 men huddled around the walls in that building, and that those gas shells are designed to penetrate an inch and a half pine plank, it's a wonder some of the convicts weren't killed or badly wounded."

The total damage of the riot was immense; an insurance agent writing up a claim for $15,000. Fortunately, Dad was a forward-thinking man who had revised the pen's insurance plan three years earlier to include riot coverage. The Idaho penitentiary was the first in the 11 western states to secure this type of coverage, good news for the state's taxpayers.

When all was said and done, Dad blamed the trouble on an attempt by a group of 11 "radicals" to take over the functions of a grievance committee. Claiming that they were placed in lockup without fair hearings, the self-proclaimed ringleaders had riled up the majority of the prison population. The warden knew he didn't have room for all 250 rioters in solitary confinement (known as Siberia), so he locked the rest in their cells indefinitely without recreation time as punishment. Of course, the 11 rabble-rousers went back to Siberia.

"The majority of the leaders have been in continuous trouble since they've been at the prison," Dad told reporters, "and some have been in lockup several times."

Dad hoped the punishment and lesson would stick but doubted it greatly. Still, for the time being, their riot had failed. The warden had prevailed.

Chapter 28

Manhunt for Kenneth Hastings

As I got older, my dad considered me strong and brave enough to assist in the manhunts when prisoners would go missing. Even on weekends when I visited my parents during and after college, I was roped into searches for escapees. It was always equally exhilarating and terrifying. I enjoyed it. It's hard to remember them all, but there were a few that stuck in my memory. They became the stories I would tell my children and grandchild whenever they asked about my life. Nothing thrilled them—or me—more than the retelling of my wild adventures tracking escaped inmates.

Kenneth B. Hastings was a convicted murderer whose sentence had been commuted from the death sentence to life imprisonment. His crime had been gruesome. Hastings and his partners-in-crime, William Owen and Ruth Sekinger, had murdered a popular local grocer while robbing the store. Owen's sentence had also been commuted to life imprisonment. Sekinger was convicted of assault with intent to commit murder and incarcerated at our women's prison.

Hastings did not look like a cold-blooded murderer. Maybe it was his wire-framed glasses, but except for his bad dental hygiene, he looked average. Nevertheless, he was calculated about his intentions, patiently watching and learning the patterns he could use to escape. He even used the benefit of the prison covering his dental care to activate his plan.

Right before his escape, Hastings had broken his leg. I think he was playing softball in the prison yard, but that detail is fuzzy. Whether Hastings' broken leg and his abundance of dental appointments were a coincidence, I don't know for sure. However, Dad and Frank O'Neil both seemed to think it would be harder for Hastings to make a run for it while they transported him to and from dental appointments. They underestimated the inmate's ambition.

After a routine post-extraction dental appointment, Hastings and O'Neil were returning to the prison by automobile. Because Hastings seemed to need crutches for any kind of mobility, he was uncuffed. An eyewitness told reporters that the prison vehicle was stopped on First Street and Jefferson when the two men inside began a physical altercation. Hastings pushed the chief deputy warden out of the car, stabbed him with a knife, and hobbled away toward a pickup truck. Seeing the knife-wielding convict getting close, the driver pushed a woman and two children out of harm's way.

Struggling with the driver, Hastings managed to get behind the wheel and jammed the truck into low gear, knocking O'Neil's car out of the way. Wounded, O'Neil caught onto the truck's door and was dragged around the corner before falling away. Despite being severely injured and badly bleeding, O'Neil managed to get into his slightly crushed prison vehicle and drive off in pursuit of Hastings.

The chase was on, setting off one of the largest manhunts in Idaho history. Hundreds of law enforcement officers and people began searching for Hastings. Helicopters were flown over the desolate areas and 18 roadblocks manned by 40 men were set up all around Boise. Smaller roads going to areas near Lucky Peak, Ruby Creek, Rocky Bar, Harris Creek and surrounding Idaho City were closed off. The entire population around Boise was unnerved as the convicted killer remained on the loose.

After about three days, the law enforcement officers found the stolen pickup truck on Robie Creek road, north of Boise in the mountains. The vehicle was parked 50 yards off the road and poorly disguised under tree limbs. Thinking Hastings might have dumped the truck several days before and that there were numerous cabins in the area, Dad knew the search team needed to be as big as possible. Home from college for a visit, I was recruited to be a part of the search team. Because I was 20 years old, Dad let me carry a gun in a shoulder holster.

"Be careful with this," Dad instructed. "It is only to be used under the strictest of circumstances."

We all gathered around the truck with our guns waiting for our instructions.

Earlier, Dad had received a call from a man who had trained bloodhounds during his employment at a southern state prison. The man had an old bloodhound named Ralph who previously hunted escaped inmates. Thinking this would be an excellent addition to the search party, Dad requested that the man and his dog be driven to the location of the stolen pickup. The old man had instructed that his dog needed to sniff something of Hastings to get the scent, so Dad brought some underwear from Hastings' cell. This was a good choice—underwear fits closely to the body and absorbs even the faintest of smells.

I often think back to the old man putting the escaped inmate's underwear onto the old bloodhound's nose; exactly as it is portrayed in the movies. After a good whiff, Ralph barked, and the handler let him go. Immediately, the dog headed downstream in a small creek, the group of searchers following. I held back a little, purposely staying behind the qualified law enforcement. But I also didn't want to miss any of the action. That all-to-familiar feeling of confliction overtook me—I was excited to be a part of this, but so scared of what might happen.

Then I saw him. Hastings stood behind a large tree.

"There he is!" I shouted. I heard a voice from behind me, someone yelled. "Shoot him!"

At that moment, I felt utter panic. Things were suddenly in slow motion. Pulling my gun from its holster, I dropped to my knees while trying to keep my eye on the escaped convict. Hastings stood with his hands raised. A deputy sheriff, with his gun pointed, ordered Hastings to lie down on the ground with his arms over his head.

"We got him," the deputy shouted. "Bring back-up now!"

By the time other law enforcement officers reached us, we had searched Hastings and had him ready for his return to prison. We had captured the notorious escapee only a quarter of a mile from the abandoned truck. Although he had removed the cast from his broken left leg with fingernail clippers, it was difficult for him to get very far.

I got into the backseat of the car with Hastings in the middle. I watched him carefully while also keeping an eye on my gun which I had placed back in its holster. Frank Boor, a detective from the Boise Police Department, sat on the other side of Hastings. Looking like a funeral procession, the law enforcement vehicles escorted our car back to the penitentiary. Nervous as I had been, I was also proud to have played a part in the capture.

I knew that the TV cameras would be at the prison when we returned and hoped they would film me with my holstered gun, so all my college friends would see me. We arrived at the prison and parked in front of the administrative building. I got out of the car triumphantly and sure enough they got a short clip of me with our prisoner. My name was even in the paper. Pride coursed through me, but I know Dad was also proud about the capture.

After spending a week in Siberia, Hastings disclosed his reasons for escaping. He told Dad that he had been dreaming at night about a fellow he had killed named Ivan Baker. In his dreams, Hastings kept seeing Baker coming at him in a wrestling crouch. Hastings then told Dad the reason behind his nightmare. It seems that Baker had been driving north toward Boise with Hastings, his girlfriend Ruth Sekinger, and William Owen. Somewhere in the desert area between Pocatello and Arco, Baker suggested to the felonious gang that Sekinger become a prostitute in order to bring more money. Baker's idea angered Hastings and the two got into a heated argument. With the car stopped for Baker to relieve himself, Hastings followed him into the desert and shot him four or five times. Hastings admitted to dragging Baker's body into a pile of sagebrush. Then, as if nothing had happened, Hastings returned to the car telling Owen and Sekinger that Baker had decided to pursue his own crimes and venture to Seattle.

The story interested my dad, so he decided to find out more by conducting an unconventional interview with Hastings. My dad asked Hastings if he would agree to using sodium pentothal—more commonly known as a truth serum. Dad invited me to go into the prison hospital with him, Hastings, and the pentothal technician. I remember Hastings becoming very sleepy and telling the same story under the truth serum. He also revealed that during the drive they had passed a nuclear fission plant between Pocatello and Arco where he had lit a cigarette before shooting Baker. Dad shared that information with the sheriff who covered the Arco area. However, a search found nothing.

Hastings died in 1965 and a couple of years later, I read in the *Idaho Statesman* about a man finding some old human bones in the area where Baker was allegedly shot. The FBI picked up the case and eventually confirmed the identity of the remains as Baker.

Several years later when I was a deputy clerk for the U.S. District Court in Boise, I received a visit from the U.S. Marshal.

"Jerry, I've got a man who says he knows you and wants to talk to you," the Marshal told me. I followed the officer to a holding cell where William Owen was awaiting some court appearance.

"I just wanted to get something off my chest," the prisoner stated.

"Kenny Hastings definitely killed Ivan Baker. There's no way it couldn't have been him."

Kenneth Hastings. (Idaho State Archives)

Chapter 29

The Last Hanging in Idaho

Back in 1951, Ernest Walrath and Troy Powell made history as the only double execution in the state of Idaho. Their hangings were the last to occur outdoors. My dad had the persistent feeling that outdoor hangings were too visible and public, causing the other inmates to be uneasy and agitated.

Even though the Idaho State Penitentiary did not have many convicts given the death penalty, Dad decided it was time to construct an indoor gallows area. Turns out that the first—and only—Idaho hanging to take place indoors was on October 18, 1957.

Raymond Allen Snowden brutally attacked and murdered 40-year-old Cora Dean on Saturday night, September 23, 1956. The next morning, her bloodied body was discovered by a Garden City paperboy. Soon after, Snowden was apprehended by Detective Frank Boor at Hannifin's Cigar Store in Boise. Employees had seen Snowden drop a knife in the gutter, then enter the store to wash blood off his hands in the restroom.

After his arrest, Snowden became known as "Idaho's Jack the Ripper." He had stabbed his victim 29 times with a pocketknife. The fatal wounds included a slashed throat and severed spinal cord.

The trial was swift. Snowden was quickly convicted of his horrible crime and his time in the prison was brief, 13 months on death row with his cell stationed directly in front of the tall gallows room where he would be hanged.

On the night of the hanging, the victim's family watched from the viewing area that was separated by glass from the gallows.

"Do you have any final words," Snowden was asked.

"Yes, I do," he grumbled, "but I don't know how to say them."

After that, the execution took a horrible turn. Usually in a hanging, the neck is snapped as the body drops. However, someone miscalculated Snowden's weight and his neck did not snap. Instead, the rope slowly, painfully strangled him. He choked and sputtered for 15 minutes before the noose finally ended his life.

I was 23 at the time of Snowden's hanging. Six years had passed since the double execution of Walrath and Powell. I had been through college and gotten more mature since that night. However, I knew nothing good would come from me witnessing the end of Snowden's life. Because of my previous experience seeing the aftermath of the last executed prisoners, I elected to be far from the gallows room that night. The image of Walrath's neck already haunted me; the sounds of Snowden's horrible death did not need to infiltrate my nightmares, as well.

Snowden was buried in an unmarked grave in the cemetery up the road from the prison stables. Ghost hunters and fans of the paranormal believe Snowden's spirit haunts the penitentiary to this day, even though it is no longer in use.

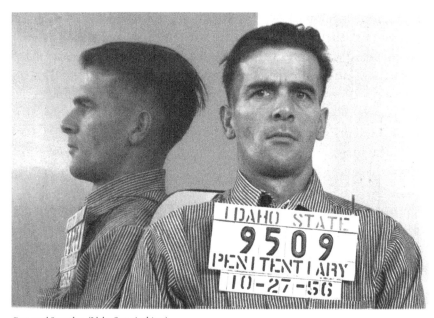

Raymond Snowden. (Idaho State Archives)

Chapter 30

Warden Calls Bluff

Five House was a cellblock that contained the most violent prisoners. Guards' Frank Zack and Howard Schraft had entered the cell house just after eight in the morning to deliver breakfast trays. Inmate Paul Mahaffry, serving two life sentences, hit Zack on the head with a piece of iron torn from a bed. Another inmate grabbed the iron weapon and hit Schraft. Taking the keys, Mahaffry released the other prisoners on the block. Using the intercom system, Mahaffry called the warden's office to announce they had hostages.

Dad rounded up 15 guards armed with rifles, shotguns, and blow torches. When they arrived at Five House, the guards began cutting through the steel doors with the blow torch.

"Warden, if you don't shut off that torch," Mahaffry yelled, "we're going to cut off the heads of these guards and roll them down the corridors like bowling balls."

"If you touch one of my guards," Dad called back, "I'll have to kill everyone in that cell block."

One of the state troopers told me that Dad handed him a Thompson submachine gun. The Trooper said he had only seen that kind of weapon in movies or comic books.

When the guards finished cutting out the door and entered the cell block, every inmate was back in their cell. Except for the initial bruises, the two guards were untouched.

Later, I asked Dad, "What would you have done if you'd found the guards had been killed?"

"Jerry", he said, "I would've unloaded it in the block, then walked out and resigned. I've never told inmates anything I wasn't fully prepared to do and they know it."

Deputy Warden Pat O'Neil and Warden Lou Clapp. (Idaho State Archives)

Chapter 31

Two in the Furnace Room

After I graduated college, got married and had children, I would often visit my parents at the penitentiary. My mother was always so excited to see her grandkids. My children were kept close to the house and were too young to understand much of the prison life. On one such visit, after dinner, Dad and I sat outside on the front steps. As we talked, a shot rang out from one of the tower guards. My father rushed into the house and called the turnkey to find out what happened. I could hear the turnkey on the other end of the line.

"Two inmates just busted out of their cells, Warden. They were trying to escape over the North wall when we caught sight of them."

Dad hung up.

"Let's go, Jerry."

Upon our arrival in the administrative building, we got all the information regarding the attempted escape. Apparently, two inmates had broken out of their cells and attacked the night guard. They attempted to escape over the North wall when one of the tower guards fired a warning shot off the wall. The two inmates then dropped from the wall and hid somewhere in the yard.

"Sorry we didn't call you first, Warden. We had to call an ambulance; we've got a badly injured guard in there."

The guard who tried to apprehend the inmates had been brutally beaten around his head and had to be taken out on a stretcher to the hospital in Boise. By this time, a number of law officers had gathered outside Dad's office, awaiting a plan to search the prison yard for the two dangerous convicts.

"We need an even number. Everyone goes in pairs," Dad commanded the group of men. "Jerry, that means you have to help out, too."

I looked for the biggest guy in the room and partnered up with him. I stayed near him as we all entered the prison yard. The large deputy sheriff and I went to the left as we all fanned out in different directions. Within a few steps, we came to a corner in front of the cafeteria.

"You go to the right," the deputy sheriff whispered to me. "I'll go left and see you around the other side."

With some apprehension, I silently nodded in agreement and proceeded to the right side of the cafeteria. I felt intense trepidation. *Two escaped inmates had just beaten a night guard nearly to death and I'm being left alone?* That first night at the prison came to mind: I felt horribly conflicted yet again. *What if these escapees try to hurt me? What will my wife and children do if I am murdered tonight? These men are obviously dangerous, but I will be a hero if I catch them.* As I moved cautiously, I noticed a door that led into the basement of the cafeteria appeared to be broken. It looked as though the top half of the door was missing. Boldly, with increased anxiety, I ventured down the outside basement stairs to the broken door. It was ajar. Upon entering the basement, I was surprised to find an inmate reclining on a cot wearing just his underwear.

"Have you had any company in here tonight?" I asked him.

"Yes," he responded, "they're around the corner waiting for you."

Indicating with a nod toward the furnace, the inmate watched as I inched closer. I slowly, quietly approached the furnace and looked around it, the two wannabe escapees standing with their hands raised. I backed up to the basement doorway, not daring to turn my back on any of the men in that room.

"I've got them," I hollered. "We're down in the basement."

My companion, as well as many others who had been searching the yard, heard my yell and rushed down the steps. The inmates were forced to strip down for a thorough body search.

I had captured the two inmates. I was anxious to see my father; I knew he would be proud.

I walked with the procession of guards, sheriffs, and two naked prisoners toward solitary confinement. But as we walked over the slightly uneven ground, one of the unclothed inmates toppled over on my left side into a prone position. Falling forward, hands cuffed and unable to stop his descent, the inmate hit his head on the concrete sidewalk. I turned to see what had caused him to fall, thinking he must have tripped over something. But what I saw was a guard with a long flashlight in his hand, an angry expression on his face. The flashlight appeared almost bent in the middle.

"That one tried to run so I hit him," I heard the guard say to another man in the group.

Someone helped the inmate up. He was very shaken, but uninjured, and so we continued our trip to the Hole. I remember feeling perturbed. Dad needed to know what had happened to that inmate, even if he wasn't injured.

When we got to my father's office there was a smattering of newspaper reporters. The guards and law enforcement officers all needed to have their say, as well. Being too distressed about the interaction between the guard and the inmate, I completely forgot about my part in the apprehension of the convicts. I sat in Dad's office and waited for everyone to leave. The last person there was the guard who had hit the inmate. I watched with thinly veiled dislike as he put the bent flashlight on my dad's desk.

"Warden, one of the inmates tried to run," the guard said matter-of- factly. "I had to hit him."

Although uneasy, I patiently waited for this man to finish his story and leave the office.

"Dad, that inmate did not try to run. That guard hit him without any reason."

Tired from the commotion, my dad let me explain my feelings about the situation. When I was finished, he looked at me square in the face.

"Jerry, do you recall the guard we had removed from the yard?"
I nodded. *Who could forget such a horrible thing so soon?*

"He's in the hospital in very serious condition," Dad continued. "He is not likely to make it through the night. If he does, he will never have a normal life again."

Dad paused.

"I would like to know how you would feel if I had been that guard that they took to the hospital tonight. The guard who left the flashlight on my desk was the brother of the hospitalized guard."

I sat there in deep thought, considering the horror.

"That inmate tried to run, Dad."

Chapter 32

Remembering Dad

The thing about my dad—he was unbelievably fair. He never lied to an inmate. He didn't like to make promises; but when he said something would happen, he would follow through. While the inmates didn't like him, per se, they respected him. And, in turn, Dad showed them the respect he felt they deserved.

"These men and women have done bad things, made poor choices," he told me. "I'm here to make sure they are trying to become better citizens."

Warden Clapp ran the prison in a way that promoted self-sufficiency. He believed that learning job skills was the best way for inmates to achieve rehabilitation.

Dad was remarkably good at reaching that target. Because he facilitated general positivity within the prison, most of the prisoners kept their heads down and did their time accordingly. He felt that so long as a person was honest with him and followed through on what they said, he would treat them the same way. It was his style of discipline and it worked . . . usually.

As an adult, I asked my dad a lot of questions about his time as warden. I was always enthralled by the stories he had either not yet shared with me or I had missed because I was away at college. I knew he was a highly capable man, but there were some instances that have never failed to solidify my belief in my father's skill at managing difficult situations.

129

I can still hear his voice.

"Jerry, is there anything you want to tell me?"

Louis Egmer Clapp, 1909-72. (Idaho State Archives)

Epilogue

Jerry compiled quite a few high school truancies, so the Clapp household was ecstatic when he graduated. He was sailing high in his world until about two weeks before he left for the University of Idaho. Euphoria turned into rage when his father decided Jerry would not be allowed to have his car for his freshman year of college. Jerry had worked hard to buy that car, but he reluctantly relinquished the keys.

Mischief was at hand during Jerry's first year away from home. Many of his fraternity brothers were veterans returning from the Korean War. Thus, his pledge class outings took a different twist from the norm. Before the football game against Washington State, they strategically charted a plan to steal their rival's mascot. Dressed in camouflage, the pledges headed down the road from Moscow to Pullman to kidnap a live cougar. Unfortunately, the local police intercepted them at the cougar's cage and some of the pledges were arrested. Jerry escaped, but felt guilty about the others and went to the jail to turn himself in. The police told him to go home.

In the spring, Jerry and a friend took dates to a dance in Lewiston, Idaho. Before returning to campus in Moscow they needed gas, but the service station refused to take a check. At a loss, Jerry's friend asked the attendant where they would be able to cash a check that time of night. It was suggested they try the local police station, but the desk sergeant refused to cash the friend's check because he did not know him. The friend pointed to Jerry.

"Will you take his check? His father is Lou Clapp."

The officer would gladly cash the check from Lou Clapp's son.

Jerry wrote the check, they bought the gas, and had their dates home before curfew.

Early Monday morning, Jerry received a phone call from his father.

"I knew you would end up in prison someday," the warden barked, "because no one writes a bum check to the police station!"

Jerry Clapp's high school senior photo. (Courtesy of the Clapp Family)

Jerry avoided jail and never again wrote a bad check.

In September 1954, Jerry married his high school girlfriend, Shirley Hire. They would have five children during their 20-plus year marriage. As a family, they spent time at the prison for holidays and other family gatherings.

Jerry worked at various jobs to provide for his family, including as a sodium pentothal technician for an alcohol rehabilitation center in Wendell, Idaho. In 1958 he found his niche in the federal court system. Jerry always credited Senator Frank Church for getting him a job as a deputy clerk. He loved every aspect of the courts and in 1973 became Clerk of the United States 9th District Court for the state of Idaho.

He had the utmost respect for all federal judges he served, acquiring a deep appreciation for the law. Jerry took immense pride in his position being, as he put it, "clerk of the great and sovereign district of Idaho." He served as President of the U.S. Court Clerks Association in 1979.

Lou Clapp continued as Warden of the Idaho Penitentiary until his retirement. In March 1966, upon the death of Edson Deal, Lou was appointed by the governor to the position of Secretary of State for Idaho. Lou continued to consult in the planning of the construction of a new prison. At the time of his death in 1972, Lou was working with an old friend subdividing and selling recreational lots within the Crown Point area in Cascade, Idaho.

Jerry took his father's place in the Crown Point project on weekends. This provided him a great opportunity to include his children in the land business. Quite often he would take a child with him while showing various lots to prospective buyers. Eventually, Jerry was able to buy lots along the way to sell for himself and his mother. In 1976, he purchased and subdivided 36 acres adjacent to Crown Point from the railroad creating the Vista Point Subdivision. He also purchased and sold the land surrounding Massacre Rock and "C" Rock.

In 1979, Jerry and I were married. About a month before our wedding date, Jerry decided we should have a trial run of combining our two families by going on a trip. So, we loaded his two youngest with my three children into a rented mobile home and set out on an adventure to Wyoming—Jackson Hole and Yellowstone. His reasoning was if we survived the trip and were still speaking, the marriage would be good. He was right. Our marriage was strong enough to raise the five children through their teenage years into adulthood.

Although we lived in Nampa, many weekends were spent in Cascade where Jerry could work the land before playing with the family in the lake. Quite often, Jerry would swing by Massacre Rock above the dam with perspective buyers incorporating a brief history of Cascade into his tour of the land. He loved to vividly tell people about the war between the settlers and the Tukudeka, or Mountain People; a subset of the Shoshone Tribe.

Jerry instilled a strong sense of honesty and a respect for the law into all of the children. Being inspired by his father, one of his sons and a granddaughter graduated from the University of Idaho with a degree in Criminal Justice. Another granddaughter graduated from the University of Idaho School of Law and is an attorney in the Eagle area.

Jerry's philosophy in life was to quit while being on top of your game. In the last few years of his career, he was the clerk of both the U.S. District Court and the Bankruptcy Court in Idaho. In the spring of 1991, he retired from the federal court system. As usual, Jerry didn't linger in the past but focused on the future, selling his land investments, building his dream home on Vista Point, meeting new friends, and lending a hand to others in need.

Jerry always carried a mischievous sense of humor and a wonderful gift for storytelling, captivating his audiences with tales of growing up at the prison. Jerry lived his life on his terms, loved people, cherished his family and friends.

– Bette Joe Clapp

Inmate Biographies

Harry Orchard (#1406)

Born: March 18, 1866 in Wooler, Ontario, Canada
Birthname: Albert H. Edward Horsley
Booking Date: March 1908 (age 42)
Crime & Sentence: Murder and hired assassin, Death (commuted to life in prison)
Victim: Frank Steunenberg, former governor of Idaho.
Time at Prison: Harry Orchard was a model inmate and trusty, spending most of his time in his own quarters outside the cell houses. He grew strawberries, plus tended to chickens and turkeys. He crafted a variety of saddlery products that he was able to sell. He also made a doll house for Jerry's sister, Pat. He wrote *Confessions and Autobiography of Harry Orchard* (1907) and *The Man God Made Again* (1952). Orchard applied for parole, but it was never granted. He served the longest sentence term in Idaho history.
Death: April 13, 1954, age 88, Idaho State Penitentiary
Note: Orchard confessed to killing 17 additional people but guessed the number might be higher. A bronze statue of his last victim—Frank Steunenberg, the fourth governor of Idaho (1897-1900)—stands in front of the Idaho State Capitol in Boise.

J. Britt Hargraves (#6160)

Born: July 8, 1914 in Pocatello, Idaho
Booking date: November 22, 1939 (age 26)
Crime & Sentence: Murder in the first degree, Life in prison
Victim: F.F. "Bob" Hunter, marshal of Alameda, Idaho
Occupations at prison: photographed incoming inmates, ballistcs work, tended to pump house, and assigned to the chief clerk's office.

Parole: March 7, 1960 after serving 21 years (final discharge from parole on September 19, 1966).

Died: November 6, 1968, Grand Island, Nebraska.

Note: Marshal Bob Hunter responded to a call made by Hargraves's wife, who had filed for divorce earlier that day and had fled to her parent's house. Hargraves was serving a two-year parole for burglary that maintained he stay away from his wife's family and not be involved with any firearms. Hargraves fatally shot Hunter, fled the scene, and hid at a construction site for a dormitory at Idaho State University. When officers encountered him, Hargraves shot one in the arm and severed the finger of the other. Hargraves turned the gun on himself but survived the shot.

Abraham Rich (#6697)

Born: December 18, 1888 in Clay Center, Kansas

Booking Date: February 2, 1937 (age 55)

Crime & Sentence: Incest, 5-10 years

Occupation at prison: Blacksmith

Escape: March 8, 1954 (he had served 401 days)

Note: A former farmer and logger in Leland, Nez Perce, Idaho, Rich had approximately nine children, with three different wives.

Arlene Lucille Daggett McWilliams (#6792)

Born: April 5, 1926 in Lincoln, Nebraska

Booking date: November 30, 1944 (age 18)

Crime & Sentence: Burglary, 1-15 years

Prior record: Having committed robbery at the age of 12, she spent two years in St. Anthony's Industrial School in Washington. She then served 1.5 years in jail for stealing from her sister. Her first husband was serving time for robbery when she met Verdelle McWilliams.

137

Paroled: October 30, 1945, to live with her parents in Seattle, Washington. She had served 11 months.

Death: Oct. 11, 2011, East Baton Rouge Parish, Louisiana.

Note: In May 1947, Verdelle McWilliams wrote to Warden Clapp asking if he knew where Arlene was so that he could divorce her. Warden Clapp wrote back that she never completed her parole in Washington, and he did not know her whereabouts. In July 1949, Warden Clapp received a letter from Arlene's father that she had been found in Texas with a husband and 10-month-old son.

Verdelle McWilliams (#6793)

Born: May 9, 1919 in Commerce, Texas

Booking date: November 30, 1944 (age 25)

Crime & Sentence: Burglary, 1-15 years

Paroled: December 1, 1945 after serving 1 year and 1 day.

Note: Prior to his incarceration in Idaho, he had served time in Texas for robbery.

Clarence "Chris" Kristiansen (#6970)

Born: August 2, 1920 in Brooklyn, New York

Booking Date: July 27, 1945 (age 24)

Crime & Sentence: Manslaughter, 6 months-10 years

Victim: Carolyn Ann Symms (8-years-old)

Release Date: August 1, 1946 after serving 11 months

Death: 1982, Elk County, Pennsylvania

William Dreyer (#5907, #5527, #5837, #6597, #8214)

Born: April 26, 1913 in Idaho Falls, Idaho

#5097 Booking date: March 31, 1935 (21 years old)

Crime & Sentence: Forgery, 1-14 years

Paroled: April 1937

Note: Dreyer, who was married, had been a dairyman.

#5527 Booking date: June 21, 1937 (age 24)

Crime & Sentence: Forgery, 1-14 years (while in jail for reckless driving, information surfaced that he had forged checks).

Paroled: November 19, 1938 "on the condition that he refrain from intoxicating liquors, observe all laws, obtain employment, lead an upright life, and report to the sheriff once a month."

Note: While incarcerated, Dreyer became a barber. He was now divorced.

#5837 Booking date: December 24, 1938 (age 25)

Crime & Sentence: Forgery, 3-14 years

Escape: December 9, 1940 from the Eagle Island Prison Farm. Arrested in Utah on April 10, 1941, receiving 1-5 additional years at the Idaho State Pen.

Paroled: April 1, 1942

#6597 Booking date: December 4, 1942 (age 29)

Crime & Sentence: Forgery, 3-14 years

Paroled: June 6, 1945

#8214 Booking date: May 4, 1951 (age 38)

Crime: Issuing a fictitious check

Paroled: July 10, 1953

Death: November 4, 1967 in Salt Lake City, Utah. He was survived by a wife, son, stepdaughter, and two grandchildren.

Note: Between 1935-53, Dreyer served 4,407 days (11 years, 1 month) in the Idaho State Penitentiary. Becoming a tinsmith, he would be arrested again in 1954. From 1960-1966, he spent time in the South Dakota State Penitentiary.

Delmar Theodore Swatsenbarg (#7241, #8376)

 Born: October 29, 1919 in Aurora, Missouri

 #7241 Booking Date: May 6, 1949 (age 29)

Crime & Sentence: Forgery, 1-14 years
Occupation at Prison: Baker (donuts at the State Pen were said to be the best in Boise)
Paroled: September 15, 1951
Note: Swatsenbarg became the prison baker. Donuts at the State Pen were said to be the best in Boise.
#8376 Booking date: February 16, 1952 (age 32).
Crime: Arrested from the incident involving penitentiary guard Lovell Painter.
Paroled: September 12, 1959. He returned October 6, 1960 for parole violation and was finally released on April 5, 1961.
Death: February 17, 1993, age 73 (Long Beach, California)
Note: Swatsenbarg stated that he was too drunk to remember the incident with Painter. He claimed that the prosecuting attorney told him that if he did not plead guilty he would be charged with robbery and kidnapping.

Verna "Tarzan" Norton Keller (#7282)
    Born: August 25, 1930 in Belfry Carbon, Montana
    Booking date: December 18, 1947 (age 17)
    Crime & Sentence: Murder in the second degree, Life in prison
    Victim: Bonnie Plaster (16 years old). The crime was committed with Keller's companion, Roscoe Hartley (age 29), who also served time at the Idaho State Pen.
    Escaped: April 1948 (with Margaret Barney) by scaling the wall with a ladder made of kindling. They had been working for several days to loosen the bar in a window of their cell house. The women told Warden Clapp, "we had been talking about escaping for a long time and we did it just to show you that we could." Lou Clapp stated, "both women treated the entire affair as a lot of fun and a great prank".
    Paroled: August 18, 1955 after serving 9 years, 8 months, 11 days.
    Death: July 3, 2002 in Santa Maria, California

Margaret Barney (#7323)

    Born: December 23, 1926 in Bristow, Oklahoma

    Booking date: February 3, 1948 (age 21)

    Crime & Sentence: Robbery, 15 years

    Escaped: April 1948 (with Verna Keller)

    Released: July 6, 1951 after serving 3 years, 5 months, 3 days.

    Note: Margaret was 14 when she married her first husband, 16 when she married again, and 20 when she moved to Idaho and married James Barney. In December 1947, the pair began breaking into houses and stealing presents under Christmas trees. They were arrested after committing an armed robbery of James Galloway, a Boise attorney. Both would serve time at the penitentiary. At Margaret's release, she was sent to live with her aunt and uncle in Oklahoma. By 1971, Margaret had remarried and was working as a maid at Cactus Pete's Casino in Jackpot, Nevada.

Troy D. Powell (#7986)

    Born: January 5, 1930 in Endicott, Nebraska

    Booking date: June 16, 1950 (age 20)

    Crime & Sentence: Murder in the first degree, Death

    Victim: Newton Wilson

    Time served: 9 Months, 29 days

    Death: Hanged, April 13, 1951, Idaho State Penitentiary

    Note: Served in the Army Air Corps (1946-47) with an honorable discharge. Incarcerated in the Oregon State prison in Salem for larceny (1948-49). A truck driver, he was married to Delphine May Walrath (Ernest Walrath's sister).

Ernest Walrath (#7987)

    Born: February 23, 1931 in Bend, Oregon

    Booking Date: June 16, 1950 (age 19)

Crime & Sentence: Murder in the first degree, Death
Victim: Newton Wilson
Death: Hanged, April 13, 1951, Idaho State Penitentiary
Note: At the age of 17, Walrath was jailed for burglary in Deschutes County (Oregon). He also served time in the Oregon State prison in Salem.

Kenneth Hastings (#8330)

Born: September 29, 1922 in Bismarck, North Dakota
Booking date: December 7, 1951 (age 29)
Crime & Sentence: Murder in the first degree, Death (commuted to life imprisonment on July 17, 1953)
Victim: Bert McCurry
Paroled: In 1963, to take care of his elderly mother.
Death: 1965, of acute alcoholism
Note: During World War II in Algeria, Hastings was injured in the line of duty. A trained machinist and mechanic, Hastings attempted several escapes, the most successful lasting 56 hours. It was later discovered that he had also murdered Ivan Baker.

William Owen (#8329)

Born: October 2, 1911 in Tan Oak, California
Booking date: December 7, 1951 (age 40)
Crime & Sentence: First degree murder, Death (commuted to life imprisonment on July 17, 1953).
Victim: Bert McCurry
Paroled: August 22, 1962 (returned in 1963 after violating parole)
Previous and future records: Owen spent time at the Preston School of Industry for grand theft (1928-30), San Quentin for burglary (1932-33), San Quentin for forgery (1936-42), San Quentin for parole violation (1942-45), and San Quentin for

robbery and parole violation (1948-51). After his release from the Idaho State Pen in 1962, he violated parole and was returned for another year. In 1969, he was arrested for bank robberies and would spend 11 years at Leavenworth Penitentiary in Kansas.

Note: Owen and Hastings spent 13 months on death row at the Idaho State Pen, housed in the two cells that Troy Powell and Ernest Walrath occupied before their executions. Before their sentence was commuted, Owen and Hastings watched as lumber was stacked up outside their cells in preparation to build the scaffolding for their hangings.

Ruth Ellen (McCormack) Sekinger (#8349)

Born: June 10, 1919 in Pocatello, Idaho
Booking Date: Dec. 29, 1951 (age 32)
Crime & Sentence: Assault with intent to commit robbery, 14 years
Paroled: January 31, 1954 after serving 3 years, 1 month, 2 days.
Death: October 6, 1993
Note: Sekinger eventually married a psychologist, had three children, and moved to Switzerland.

Raymond Snowden (#9509)

Born: October 22, 1921 in Middleboro, Massachusetts
Booking date: October 27, 1956 (age 35)
Crime & Sentence: Murder in the first degree, condemned to hang on December 7, 1956. He appealed and the date was delayed to October 18, 1957. In all, he was incarcerated at the State Pen for 11 months and 21 days.
Victim: Cora Lucyle Dean
Death: By hanging on October 18, 1957. It would be the only hanging at the prison to take place in the indoor gallows.
Note: Starting at the age of 12, he was sent to Lyman School for

Boys multiple times for various crimes, including breaking and entering. After working with a traveling carnival, he joined the military in 1941, but was dishonorably discharged in 1942 after being arrested for going AWOL. He would find work as a laborer. His first wife divorced him, and second wife had him arrested for assault. Two weeks before he stabbed Cora Dean to death, he beat his girlfriend so badly that he broke her ribs and knocked out teeth. She called the police but dropped charges. After his arrest, he would admit to stabbing two other women, but conclusive information was never obtained.

Guard Biographies

Paris "Pat" O'Neil

Born: April 5, 1886 in Phillipsburg, Montana

Record: A former deputy sheriff in Lemhi county, Pat came to the Idaho State Penitentiary in 1932 and was appointed Deputy Warden 1934. During World War II he left to serve as captain of the guards at Swan Island Shipyards. Pat O'Neil served roughly 24 years at the State Pen and had a track record of successfully catching escaped convicts. "It was often Pat," wrote Jerry Clapp, "who would knock on our door to alert my dad of any problems within the prison walls."

Death: December 10, 1956 while still serving at the Penitentiary. Lou Clapp was one of the pallbearers at the funeral.

Frank O'Neil

Born: November 19, 1891 in Phillipsburg, Montana

Record: The Associate Warden and younger brother of Pat O'Neil, Frank served at the Idaho State Penitentiary for 38 years (1927-65).

Death: July 1969, Boise, Idaho

Bob Hawon Stubblefield

Born: July 27, 1878 in Carroll County, Arkansas

Record: The Stubblefield family moved to Oregon in 1883, his cousin, Frank Stubblefield, founding the town of Enterprise. Working in the mining and timber industries, Bob joined law enforcement in 1925, he was a deputy sheriff in Grangeville, Idaho, before coming to Boise in 1936. Starting as a guard, he was promoted in 1946 by Lou Clapp to oversee the Bull Gang on Eagle Island. "Big Bob" Stubblefield served at the Idaho State Penitentiary for 19 years.

Death: November 17, 1955, heart attack while working with inmates in the poultry sheds at Mosley Ranch.

Merritt Woodson Lavender

Born: September 25, 1888 in New Castle, Virginia

Record: Moving to Idaho in 1920, he worked for the Lewiston Police department until 1938, when he became a guard at the State Pen in Boise. He became the turnkey in 1941. His son was in a Japanese Prisoner of War camp from May 1942 until his liberation in October 1945.

Death: May 2, 1968, Boise, Idaho.

Index

Made in the USA
Las Vegas, NV
22 April 2025